Informal Learning

Informal Learning

A New Model for Making Sense of Experience

LLOYD DAVIES

Routledge
Taylor & Francis Group

LONDON AND NEW YORK

First published 2008 by Gower Publishing

2 Park Square, Milton Park, Abingdon, Oxon OX14 4RN
711 Third Avenue, New York, NY 10017, USA

Routledge is an imprint of the Taylor & Francis Group, an informa business

First issued in paperback 2016

British Library Cataloguing in Publication Data
Informal learning : a new model for making sense of experience
1. Experiential learning
I. Davies, Lloyd
153.1'524

ISBN 978-0-566-08857-5 (hbk)
ISBN 978-1-138-25626-2 (pbk)

Library of Congress Cataloging-in-Publication Data
Davies, Lloyd, 1935-
Informal learning : a new model for making sense of experience / by Lloyd Davies.
p. cm.
Includes bibliographical references and index.
ISBN 978-0-566-08857-5
1. Experiential learning. I. Title.

BF318.5.D38 2008
370.15'23--dc22

2008003938

Contents

List of Figures

List of Boxes

Preface

My purpose in writing this book is to help its readers to learn from their experiences. Everyone learns from experience, yet it is very rare for us to have a clear idea of how that learning takes place, of what mental processes are involved. In one respect, this is hardly surprising: our first learning as a newly born child is from our experiences of our mother and our environment, and by the time we start school, where learning is often thought to begin, the *tabula rasa*, the 'clean sheet' of our young minds has learned an enormous quantity of data. We know who we are, where we live, how to get around in our home and the areas outside, who a wide range of people are, quite possibly from the very old to the very young, about plants, animals, how to behave, to influence other people and so on.

Almost all of this has been learned by experience, using all our five senses to acquire data and by developing some mental models for processing that data so that, for the most part, it makes sense and can be used. The learning we encounter at school over the next dozen years or so is arguably small compared with the first few years' development of practical knowledge.

This is not to argue that adults learn from experience in the same way as do young children. Adults often have prior knowledge, gained from previous experiences and/or formal education, which assist – or sometimes may impede – learning, whereas a child generally has no preconceptions. However, it does help to explain why adults are uncertain about how they learn from experience, from everyday, or sometimes quite exceptional, events. They are tapping into a personal process which they have used for, literally, the whole of their lives, and it is not surprising that their awareness of a process that started the moment they were born, and possibly even earlier when in the womb, is dim.

Yet if you ask adults how much of what they know and use in their normal lives, at work and during leisure, is derived from experience as compared with formal knowledge, that is material they have learned from textbooks, lectures, newspapers, the TV and so on, experience wins hands down. The abilities to read and write, to do arithmetic, and perhaps to apply some simple logic, were taught at school, but beyond this for some people experience was the only teacher. Even for people who have professional skills, such as engineers, lawyers, doctors, technologists and so on, whose store of taught knowledge is relatively great, experience is usually reported as providing well over half of what they need to know to do their jobs.

So some understanding of how experiences provide usable knowledge seems worth acquiring. Worth acquiring because different components or elements in the learning process can be strengthened and used more effectively, thus increasing the value of the knowledge learned.

GENERAL, NOT SPECIFIC

The learning process described in this book is general in the sense that it applies to a wide range of experiences, rather than being specific to particular disciplines. Many professions, such medicine, law and engineering, have over the years developed sophisticated and comprehensive methods for gaining data and working with it. These are often in the form of algorithms, step-by-step methods for solving problems, which by asking questions of increasingly specific nature are intended to lead to an answer. Thus a patient presenting to their doctor with symptoms of stomach ache will be asked a series of yes/no questions designed to eliminate major areas of the abdomen; the patient will be asked to point to the area affected (people are generally very accurate when indicating the location of a sensation), and if it is the stomach area, to describe the symptoms. If these are a sensation of indigestion an hour or two after meals the doctor may suspect an infection of *H. pylori*, and would then ask a few more increasingly specific questions to confirm this diagnosis.

The model of learning from experience, or *experiential learning*, as it is often called, that I am putting forward in this book is, by contrast, general in nature. This is because it has been derived from a wide variety of experiences described by practitioners in a range of disciplines. Some experiences were concerned primarily with people, with interrelationships, whilst others were with things, or systems, or all three. The domains of knowledge from which practitioners drew in order to learn were very wide, and the ways in which they dealt with that knowledge quite varied. So the model of experiential learning which emerged from my studies is correspondingly general, and I am encouraged to put it forward because 'new readers', people who come fresh to it and test it against their own practice of making sense from experience, say 'yes, that is pretty much how I do it'.

Although it is in no way intended to supplant the established ways of using data which professionals customarily use, the model may nevertheless be of value to them in activities outside their specific professions. Thus a doctor, for example, reflecting on an experience with the supplier of drugs or equipment, or a lawyer trying to learn from an organizational problem in the office, might find the model of help in challenging some of his or her expectations, in widening the data available for consideration, and in progressively working towards some general precepts which enable them to deal with similar situations more effectively in the future.

RESEARCH METHODS

How did I come up with this way of looking at experiential learning? The short answer is by reading quite widely and asking a lot of questions, as part of a doctoral programme at Lancaster University's Business School. Although the subject of adult experiential learning *per se* seems relatively under-researched, there is a lot of material in the related fields of adult learning, cognitive psychology, creativity and neuroscience.

Because of my background in human resource management, the type of person I was most able to interview was someone with an organizational background. My research colleagues worked in a wide span of activities, and I was able to listen to more than 30 men and women talking about their experiences in the worlds of operations, finance, marketing, academia, strategic planning, general management, training and technical services. They worked in organizations ranging from solo enterprises to large beaurocracies, private and public sectors, profit-making and not for profit, including charities, in the UK and USA. The experiences they described included events which lasted only a few minutes to others which extended over many months into years.

Slightly more than half of these individuals agreed to be interviewed on the experiences of 'exceptional events' of their choosing. I asked them to focus on exceptional events because generally speaking such events are memorable, and the 'lessons' from them are readily described. My interviews were relatively unstructured because I wanted to follow their events and their ways of looking at them.

Exceptional events could be good or bad, welcome or unwelcome. The good ones included working on new activities for a period of time, working with new colleagues with new ways of looking at things, visiting and studying their field in another, radically different country or environment. The bad events were those which they would have preferred had not happened, such as natural disasters affecting their work, strikes affecting supplies, the sudden

death of a significant colleague, or changes in the organization which brought
new and severe strains.

   As I carried out these interviews over a few years, and in parallel carried out
reading in the fields mentioned above, several themes or elements of learning
began to emerge. For example, I was struck by the emotion with which many
respondents described events which might have happened a long time ago,
perhaps even decades earlier, but which still meant much to them. Very often the
experience was a clear case of the respondent's expectations *not* being fulfilled.
As they sought to make sense of the events, they drew on several essentially
different sources of data: their own personal recollections and impressions were
naturally pre-eminent, but they took on board the views of other people in the
same event, related the event to others which they had read about or studied,
and of course drew on their own experience, where appropriate, of similar
situations. Quite often their first attempts at sense-making were unsatisfactory,
and they went back to look for more and different data before coming up with
some lessons which were credible and could be used in the future.

   After about four years of this type of interview, and several tentative
attempts at putting together a model which embraced these various elements,
I felt I had a draft which could be tested. So I then wrote a case study about a
research director who, when opening a new laboratory, had a bad experience
of upsetting the residents in the neighbourhood of the laboratory, (this drew on
several threads of my own experience) which, using the model in its latest form,
showed how and what he learned when he reflected on the event. I sent this
to a different group of respondents, 13 in all, and invited them to be critical of
the model, seeking comments about omissions, duplications, and any aspects
which did not capture their own ways of making sense of experiences.

   Finally, after publishing my doctoral thesis, I explored certain aspects in
workshops at the University of Lancaster and elsewhere with groups of people
who were studying the processes of learning.

   It can thus be seen that I have had the benefit of several fairly different types
of contribution, from interviewees, commentators and participants in group
discussions, not to mention numerous individuals who have shown interest in
this work. For the sake of brevity, in the following chapters they are referred to
as *research colleagues*.

   I do not offer this work with any suggestion of it representing the final
version of the ways in which people learn from their experiences, because all

aspects of it would benefit from further, more detailed exploration. However, it appears to be more comprehensive than the models of learning already published, and as such a small step forward in understanding this type of learning. By focusing on the various elements of the process, my hope is that readers in a wide range of occupations will find it helpful when considering their own experiences, and seeking to use the lessons derived from them in the future.

NOTES AND REFERENCES

Because this book is intended for a general, rather than academic, readership, I have not burdened the main text with references, nor gone into the extent of detail which students might expect. However, for the benefit of the latter, I have sought to expand certain areas in the footnotes in each chapter, and to include in the Bibliography at the end of the book sufficient detail to enable the interested reader to follow up particular points.

WATERAID

Any royalties from the sale of the book will be given to WaterAid, a British charity set up to assist communities in developing countries to help themselves with the provision of clean water, the disposal of sewage and water-related health education. Many people in the British water industry support WaterAid, probably as a result of their recognition of the importance of water as an absolutely basic condition of a healthy and productive life, and I have seen the benefits which villages or small communities can create for themselves given some financial help and practical guidance. This approach seems to be an essential part of the strategy for tackling the world's water problems.

My observation, moreover, is that WaterAid is an interesting example of an organization which learns from its experience. The sharing of knowledge of techniques between different countries, and the formal reviews intended to assess the effectiveness of WaterAid-assisted schemes, have echoes, at the organizational level, of many of the processes described later in this book which lead to learning from experience.

More information on the work of WaterAid can be obtained from the Chief Executive, WaterAid, 47–49 Durham Street, London, SE11 5JD.

Acknowledgements

Many people have contributed to this book. They include my 'research colleagues', that is those who shared their experiences with me and contributed to my ideas on experiential learning, and whose actual or paraphrased words run through the text like stars in the Milky Way; friends and acquaintances who listened patiently as I described my emerging conceptions and offered constructive comments; those who gave practical and invaluable assistance helping me over some of the hurdles of actual production, of the thesis and now this book; and my family, whose studied stance of benign neglect gave me the space to indulge another mild eccentricity. Without them my research and this book could not have been accomplished.

For me this work has been like a journey, and all those listed below have helped me on my way. My sincere thanks go to them all. My research colleagues cannot be named because I assured them of anonymity before they vouchsafed their experiences. Their names have been changed, but their words and their wisdom remain to be read in the following chapters. Others I am anxious to identify because the valuable assistance they gave so willingly deserves it.

First in the list, and first in the journey, is my Supervisor at Lancaster, Professor Michael Reynolds, who steered my through the, to me, arcane world of academic research, and I am delighted to record my thanks. My friend and former colleague Anne Twigg gave much time and expertise preparing my thesis ready for binding. Julian Tippett gave truly invaluable assistance in preparing the many versions of the Model and other illustrations ready for printing. Ken Allison, Judith Barras, Jayne Mothersdale and Alan Mumford read early versions of this book and made very helpful constructive criticisms. Jeff Gold was a steadfast friend throughout the whole journey from research to publication, offering perceptive advice, initially on what academics are looking for, and later on what publishers are looking for. Finally, Jonathan Norman and his colleagues have taken the book through the various stages of publication, all new to me, efficiently and painlessly.

It gives me real pleasure to make formal recognition of each of these friends and colleagues. They have contributed to the book's content, its shape and appearance, and more than that they have contributed, through their encouragement and explicit and generous support, to my sense of well-being. It has been a pleasure to work with each of them.

CHAPTER 1

Introduction

WHAT IS THIS BOOK ABOUT?

Everybody learns from experience. Cats and dogs do it, and for humans it is our first form of learning, arguably starting while we are still in the womb and observable from the first few hours after birth. During the early years of life until we start school, experience is much the greatest teacher, when we do things ourselves and we watch the consequences of what other people do. From then onwards, well into normal old age, our actions and thoughts are influenced by our experiences.

Jeannie's Sense of Shame and Inadequacy

Jeannie has a demanding job running a GP's practice. One day, totally unexpectedly, in the surgery waiting room she met a friend, A, from school days, who was visiting the doctor because of a family tragedy. 'I wasn't prepared for A coming in, and I came out of the office and saw her, and I discovered I simply didn't know what to say. I just went back into my office; I felt as though I'd let A down, and let myself down. I felt ashamed, really, that I couldn't even speak.'

'That's what set me thinking, that here was a situation I was totally out of my depth in. How could I work on something to make it so that I wasn't like that any more? Or for the girls in the Practice as well?'

This is an experience, mercifully not an everyday one, which Jeannie (not her real name), described to me.[1] It obviously had a powerful impact on her, and the feelings of shame and inadequacy associated with it will probably last for many years. Happily, it had a positive outcome, as we shall see later.

If, as I have often done, you ask able and successful people how much of what they do is derived from their formal learning, from books, lectures, articles and so on and how much is rooted in their experiences, they will

---

1   As part of my research I held interviews and discussions with about 30 people, of whom Jeannie was one. Throughout this book there are references to these discussions, although in every case, to preserve the confidentiality I promised, names and other identifiable details have been changed.

almost invariably attribute a high proportion to experience. So if learning from experience is clearly significant, and people are clearly able to accomplish it, why write about it?

The answer is twofold: first, perhaps because it is so instinctive, people are generally unaware of how they do it. Secondly, this unawareness makes it unlikely that they will seek to do it better.

Working with able, professional people, and asking them how they have learned from a recent, important experience, has almost always evoked a look of blank incomprehension, as though the words 'How have you learned?', while making sense individually, make no sense when drawn together in a sentence. Very often, the question 'What have you learned?' has been difficult to answer, and has required some time to articulate what has gone wrong, or right, why that happened, and how it could be avoided, or built upon, another time. Yet this was not because they were unthinking, unlearning individuals – my longer-term observations were that they used experience effectively to improve future performance – it was only because they had never paused to consider how they did it, much less how they could do it even more effectively.

This is not only my observation. Many researchers in this field comment on the fact that even when *learning from doing* is the subject of particular study, the 'learning' aspect comes a very poor second to the 'doing'. In one article, summing up their experience that 'Working is about working, and learning about learning', two writers say 'It became obvious that the participants' focus was very much on their work and hardly at all on learning in relation to work.'[2]

Perhaps a reason for this is that most people in the developed world regard 'learning' as a formal, structured process. The teacher, lecturer, or author has thought about what he or she wants to convey to us, the 'learners', and our job is, as far as possible, to assimilate the facts, ideas or skills which the former are imparting. From the age of about 6, for 10 to 15 or more years, success in learning is generally measured by how comprehensively the learner has remembered, and can use, what the teacher had in mind. In recent years, teaching methods have mitigated this approach to some extent, but the fact remains that most learning is teacher-centred and led, including the methods by which it is achieved. (As the author of this book, I am conscious that I am saying things the ways I want to. My consolation is that I am attempting to

---

2   Keursten and Streuner (2007), page 172.

meet my readers' needs as far as possible, and am offering a way of learning that liberates the learner from a heavily prescribed way of doing things.)

So if we are asked what we have learned, and how we learned it, the natural response is probably to think back to a source of authority, a person, book or newspaper, and recount facts or ideas that have stuck in our minds. They are, probably, neatly presented and, if we have a good memory, relatable pretty much as they were presented.

Learning from experience is very different. *We* decide what lessons we have learned, and *we* decide how to relate them to someone else, how to use them in the future and how to decide whether they are successful. Indeed, *we* decide if we are going to learn anything at all. Thus Jeannie, in the example above, was prompted to find ways of relating to bereaved people; it was her decision in the first place to devote time and energy to exploring the subject, by asking other people who had substantial experience in this field, and broadening her search into a study of how other races and religions deal with death.

In a busy, sometimes hectic, life we may have no time to look back at an experience, and thus overlook whatever lessons it may have for us.

WHO IS IT FOR?

Just as learning from experience is a general phenomenon, this book is intended for the general reader.[3] More specifically, it is for people who, in managing their lives, want to make the best use of their experiences in order to re-enforce good outcomes and avoid bad outcomes.

This last sentence could usefully be elaborated. *Managing their lives* implies dealing with both the normal incidents of living, relatively routine patterns, and with the slightly, or very, exceptional events which come along to surprise us, pleasurably or to our discomfort. What do these events mean? Why were they caused? How could they happen again? *Make the most of their experiences* means seeking answers to these questions. It means digging into the origins of the experience, both in terms of what happened 'out there', that is in the outside

---

3   Although meeting the needs of the general reader is my principal purpose, I am conscious that the subject of experiential learning is of increasing interest in further and higher education, whose courses often include resort to Learning Contracts or Learning Statements as a means of enhancing the learning process. The needs of students of the subject will, therefore, be catered for in the footnotes which will elaborate the contents of most chapters. In particular, the footnotes will point to references which support the main text and provide suggestions for further reading.

world, but also into how we perceived the experience, our expectations, our emotions and our particular ways of looking at things.

Re-enforce good outcomes and avoid bad outcomes means being willing to do things differently in the light of the lessons from the experience. We would want to repeat good outcomes, satisfactory or pleasurable results, so we would look for the recipe for success. Even more so, we would want to avoid bad outcomes: if some experience has hurt us, physically or emotionally, we naturally want to find ways of avoiding putting ourselves in similar situations in the future. A child touching a hot object recoils with pain: he or she will look to see what was special about that object – near a fire, or out in a very hot sun, for example – and conclude that objects near fires or in hot suns should be approached warily. At a much more adult level, Jeannie took her sense of failure and used it to develop some new skills for future use.

It should be said at the outset that the ideas in this book, although of general application, are not necessarily universal. Some professions may have very specific ways of learning from experience; doctors, for example, have well-developed procedures when working with patients for establishing possibly causes of presented symptoms, and lawyers follow predefined routes when planning to work on a particular case in the context of relevant statute or case law. The contents of this book are not addressed to people who are following particular disciplines. This is not to say, however, that a doctor or a lawyer, faced with making sense of an experience outside their disciplines, may not find the approach helpful.

Another situation in which this book may not be immediately relevant is that where a person's experience is so awful, so traumatic, that in the short run they simply cannot face it. The ideas in this book were developed as a result of my discussions on learning from experience with people who had had 'normal' – although often unusual – experiences, and from reading various literatures on normal learning. I consciously avoided the traumatic and the abnormal, not because of a lack of interest in the subject, but because there seemed enough work to do with learning from more ordinary, commonplace, experiences.

WHAT IS AN EXPERIENCE?

In the previous paragraph one kind of experience has been explicitly excluded, although it may well be that as time passes such an experience could become open to examination and thus a potential source for learning.

The types of normal experience which *are* the subject of this book, however, cover an enormously wide span. Dictionary definitions of 'experience' typically contain phrases like 'practical acquaintance with any matter gained by trial' and 'the passing through any event or course of events by which one is affected'. From these, it is worth emphasizing two common characteristics of learning from experiences – their active nature, and that they are personal.

They are *active* in the sense that they involve the learner in something more than remembering what someone else has said. The child touching something hot, and in our earlier example, Jeannie, was prompted to learn a new skill in order to avoid future shame and embarrassment. Both engaged the learner in various mental processes before they could feel satisfied that they had learned what they thought was needed.

They are also *personal* to the extent that experiences can have very different impacts on different people, and the learning is commensurately different. Another person in Jeannie's place on the morning of her encounter could have been quite familiar with meeting bereaved people, and for that person the encounter would be normal and much less memorable. Or that other person could have had a different personality, lacked Jeannie's sensitivity to her situation, and simply not noticed it. Or take another example; two people are in a kitchen when a fire starts. One of them, who has never experienced the smoke and heat, may almost panic and would certainly remember it, whilst for the other, say a professional firefighter, the event could be forgotten almost immediately.

Two other features also add to the varieties of 'experience', and thence to the processes of learning from them. The *time span* can be very short or very long, or anything in between. A skid in a car could last for a fraction of a second, but could nevertheless provide a significant learning experience. At the other extreme, some experiences can last for months or years; people who lived through the Second World War can talk of their wartime experience – which lasted six years. In reality, of course, this was really a series of experiences, such as, if you joined the Army, meeting a bunch of very different people, being trained in new skills, the fear (and perhaps, exhilaration) of combat, the loss of comrades, and the problems of re-entry to civilian life afterwards. If you were a civilian, your experiences could be those of rationing, air raids, a completely different news regime, numerous restrictions, the loss of friends and relatives, and so on. It is hardly surprising that for most people who lived through the Second World War it provided pivotal learning experiences which influenced the rest of their lives. However, such people are usually inclined, after the passage of five or six decades, to refer to their 'wartime experience', bundling the lessons of the disparate events into a whole under the general, but very distinctive, label of being caused by 'war'.

Of course, to some extent the 'length' of an experience is a matter of definition. The few seconds of Jeannie's encounter with her friend could be regarded as 'the experience', but actually it was the trigger of a much longer process in which Jeannie did a lot of work over many months to find ways of handling that and comparable situations, yet she would probably embrace the whole as a single learning experience.

The other feature of experience is its range of complexity. Some experiences are straightforward, simple and carry straightforward and simple lessons. They are often the result of failure to do things – such as not putting a bailer in a dinghy when sailing, forgetting to water tender plants, omitting to take anti-mosquito sprays on holiday. (These are a few of my least favourite things.) In a cause–effect analysis, the experience is the effect, and the cause all too easy to identify.

Other experiences are intrinsically complex and multidimensional, and the lessons from those experiences consequently hard to discern. Disasters in machines such as aircraft are sometimes the product of the coincidence of three or four quite separate conditions combining, for example poor design, inadequate maintenance, adverse weather conditions and operator error. Two or even three of these contributors might have allowed a relatively normal flight, but the addition of the fourth tipped it into catastrophe. Learning the lessons of a disaster of this type is inevitably a long and complex process. More personal experiences, such as a row between colleagues or friends, might be difficult to analyse: was someone under unusual strain? Was the subject contentious? Was someone settling an old score? Were there other factors of which we were unaware?

THE SHAPE OF THIS BOOK

When we add up the possible variables in learning from experiences – that they require action, they are personal, they can be of any length and complexity – it is hardly surprising that a formula for analysis is difficult to discern. The fact that, nevertheless, we have been doing so, generally quite successfully, for longer than we can remember, adds to the tendency simply to accept the learning process as it is, and not to dig into it. 'If it ain't broke, don't fix it' sums up this approach.

It is my belief that some understanding of the various elements in learning from experience, or *experiential learning* as it is sometimes called, would enable us to improve the process. In the following chapters I am therefore putting forward a way of looking at experiential learning, a Model identifying the elements and pointing to some of the dynamics which, my research suggests, describes the ways people adapt to derive to useful lessons from the events in their lives.

In the next chapter, I look at some of the work that has already been carried out in this field, and Chapter 3 gives an overview of the Model. Chapters 4 to 8 look at the 'infrastructure of reflection', those features which are personal to ourselves and which influence the way we look at an experience. These help to account for the probability that if you and I went through the same event we would draw different conclusions from it – because we see it in different ways.

Chapters 9 and 10 deal with the experience itself, and our various sources for gathering data about it. Obviously, we have our own impressions, but these can be increased and enlarged by the views of those who were also involved in the same experience. A different, and potentially rewarding, perspective can be available from someone whose wasn't present, but who has seen that type of event many times and learned ways of looking that could be productive. For many experiences, especially those that involve the physical world, there is already a body of knowledge which, when we tap into it, provides useful, sometimes essential, data, which helps our understanding of the experience; I think of this as 'formal knowledge'. Finally, on the data available to help us, there is our own experience. The experience itself may be a one-off event 'out there', but the probability is that we are able to compare and contrast it with other experiences we have encountered.

Chapter 11 takes us to the heart of the sense-making processes. Given who we are and what we can learn about an experience from a variety of sources, this chapter looks at the activities of reflection, which is active rather than passive, at the ways of gaining insights and, in Chapter 12, the ways of checking our conclusions to ensure that they are sustainable and credible.

The last chapter suggests some ways of using this model of experiential learning, as an individual, in a group, and as part of mentoring or counselling processes.

The French writer Marcel Proust (1923) said 'The real voyage of discovery consists not in seeking new landscapes, but in having new eyes.' I hope that some of the contents of this book will help, by offering new insights into how we learn from experience, to provide 'new eyes' to see more from our voyages of discovery.

CHAPTER 2

Earlier Writers

INTRODUCTION

The general tone of the last chapter, in which I conveyed my observations that people generally have little access to their own ways of learning from experience, may make it seem unlikely that there is much of interest on the subject in the public domain. This is true in terms of the volume of experiential learning compared with pedagogic, that is formal, taught learning. The latter has been researched extensively and is the subject of many books and papers, and quite understandably constitutes a central part of teacher training courses.

By comparison, the experiential learning literature appears to be relatively thin, and is widely distributed between different disciplines such as education and psychology. Moreover, there generally appears to be little cross-over between disciplines; for example, Kolb, a major writer in the field of education, whose work will be discussed below, is typically not quoted in texts on cognitive psychology. This is generally because academic disciplines have their own philosophies, bodies of knowledge and research methods, and their practitioners are often reluctant to move outside them and embrace the work of others. My background, by contrast, was not rooted in any particular branch of study, and I felt able to take as wide-ranging a perspective as the subject seemed to merit, drawing on a number of disciplines.[1]

This chapter is therefore devoted to some of the work of earlier writers whose thinking has influenced my own. Each of the following authors has put forward their ideas on experiential learning in the form of a sequence, a model, of essentially different mental activities which to some extent contribute to the formulation of 'lessons' of experience. (Of course, some experiences are too complex to submit to the production of lessons, at least in the short term. Such experiences may be forgotten, or mentally filed as 'incomprehensible'; in the

---

1   Taking an eclectic approach brought some serious risks against which I had to guard. For example, drawing together the conclusions of research which was based on numerate studies following a relatively positivist approach, on the one hand, and studies based on qualitative interviews using a phenomenological approach, on the other, had to be done with caution, and a significant part of my thesis was devoted to such questions of methodology. Helpful books on this subject were Bryman's *Quantity and Quality in Social Research* (1988), and *Naturalistic Inquiry* by Lincoln and Guba (1985).

latter cases, it may be that further information or insights reveal underlying truths or conclusions, which can be used to inform further action or thought.)

It is sometimes helpful to illustrate the working of a generalized model by showing how it applies in a real case, so the box below relates an actual experience which Jim, an engineer, told me.

Jim's Difficult Meeting

Jim was responsible for introducing a bonus scheme into his department, after it had been negotiated for the company as a whole. He had to work out the details as they would apply for his staff, and negotiate them with the union branch. This is how he described the first meeting:

'This was really the first time I had been involved in this scenario – understanding the scheme, making sure it was right, how did it work, how it would affect the lads, and how we would sell it to them. And it was the first time I had dealt with the union reps; Sam (the HR Manager) helped me, but I found it a hell of an experience. Lots and lots I did wrong! Lack of planning – I'm going to say this, what will their reaction be? I was naive, thinking "well I'll think on my feet". Going into those situations you have to think on your feet, but you're helped by planning and preparation beforehand, and I didn't do enough. I was crucified! I was made to look a gibbering idiot. I remember everything I said they countered, and they countered it very well. At one stage I just didn't know the answers; Sam was trying to help me, but I thought "O God, never again, I'll never allow myself to get into this situation again."'

This experience taught Jim the importance of considering how his messages, spoken or written, would be received by their intended audience, anticipating their reactions and planning accordingly.

Later in his career, Jim held very senior positions which required him to communicate with a wide range of people – customers, suppliers, shareholders, the press and the local community. The lessons of that first negotiating meeting were applied on countless occasions.

KOLB'S EXPERIENTIAL LEARNING CYCLE

David Kolb is perhaps the best-known writer in this field, and his 1984 book *Experiential Learning* has been very influential. He offered a useful definition of learning:

> *Learning is the process whereby knowledge is created through the transformation of experience.*[2]

This definition serves well throughout this book. Building on the work of others,[3] he put forward a model of learning from experience which consists of four discrete phases, as illustrated in Figure 2.1.

Concrete experience is our perception of what actually happens, as conveyed by all our senses. Usually, of course, it will be *our* experience, but it could also be our observation, or hearing or reading, about someone else's experience; as the saying goes, 'wise men learn from the experience of others'. However, we are normally concerned with events in which we played a part, so we draw on what we did, saw, heard, felt – in both the tactile and emotional meanings – smelt and tasted. The last two would not be relevant in many experiences, but if we are learning in the kitchen, which in my own experience is a great source of learning, they can be very important. Our perceptions of an experience can sometimes be supplemented by those of others who were in the same event, as we shall see later.

So for Jim, in the experience described in earlier, the initial concrete experience was the meeting with his union reps when he found that what he was proposing to them was unacceptable, and his feelings of embarrassment, shame and inadequacy. The fact that he could describe it in great detail more than 20 years afterwards conveys something of the impact it had on him at the time.

Reflective observation means attentive consideration, pondering, mulling over and generally thinking about the experience. It is usually an active process, reviewing what has happened, seeing how strands fit together, looking harder at apparent anomalies and possibly searching for missing parts. In Jim's case, it meant reviewing the ways in which his presentation of his case had been made and the ways in which it had been received; he thought about what he had

---

2   Page 38 of *Experiential Learning*, which, incidentally, has the heading 'Experience as the source of learning and development'.

3   Kolb acknowledges the work of Dewey, Lewin and Piaget.

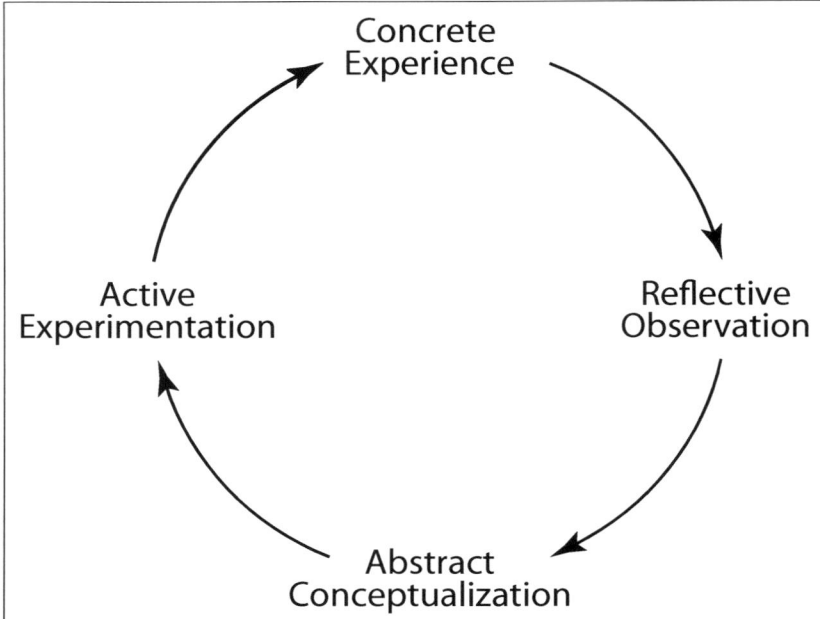

Figure 2.1   Kolb's model of experiential learning

done beforehand in preparation, and what he had not done, how his colleagues had tried to help but how in practice it was really down to him.

Abstract conceptualization could alternatively be called 'generalizing' or 'drawing conclusions'. It draws on the points which have emerged during the reflection phase and seeks to make some general sense from them, to learn the lessons which that particular experience offered. For Jim, the lessons were that people will not necessarily accept things the way he presents them; that they will look at his proposals from *their* point of view, and see them in the context of their backgrounds, experience and ideas about the future; that, as well as preparing what he wants to say, he needs to think about how the proposals he is making are likely to be received; that this possible reception should therefore influence how he makes his proposals; and that all this preparation is down to him, although he could seek help from others when doing so.

Active experimentation is really the testing out of the lessons, or concepts, which the previous phase has produced. The word 'active' is significant, implying that the conclusions or lessons drawn during the previous phase should be tested proactively to check that they are appropriate and 'right'. So Jim prepared for his next meeting with the union reps by working out in his mind what he needed to say to convince them of the merits of his arguments. In this particular instance he knew fairly well what they thought because at the first meeting they had told him (very forcefully!), and in the event he was able to allay their fears.

However, in our example it was stated that the lessons from this meeting conveyed to Jim some general truths about communication, which had application in a wide range of situations, when talking to suppliers, customers and so on. Jim was thus able to 'actively experiment' with his conclusions on communication when, in later years, he was talking to these other people. Part of the significance of the union meeting for Jim, contributing to its importance in his own development, was the fact that he found the lessons of the meeting to have virtually universal application. Whenever he was talking, or writing, to anyone in the future he had in mind the basic lesson: how will my words be received?

Helpful though Kolb's cycle is in illuminating the ways in which we learn from experience, in my view it presents only a partial picture of the various elements that are usually involved. He presents the experiential learning cycle as a neat, sequential set of activities, with one phase leading into another. For some experiences it may, indeed, be like this. For example, if you come into a kitchen and touch something, say a tin standing next to a saucepan of boiling water, and are burned by it (concrete experience), you may wonder if it has just been removed from the saucepan – is it steaming? is there a reason why it might have recently been in the saucepan? (reflective observations), and conclude that, as a general rule, it is safer to be wary of touching things in a kitchen unless you know about them (abstract conceptualization). You would probably apply this rule in the future, and find that it helped you to avoid pain (active experimentation).

However, many experiences are not so simple. The event might take much longer than the touching of a tin can, unfolding over hours or days or even longer, rather than a second or two. The context may be much more complex and multidimensional, involving different people with differing motives, physical objects, interactions of various kinds between people and/or things and so on. Making sense of experiences like these (and 'making sense' is closely related to 'learning' in real life), is rarely a neat, sequential process. Rather than progressing tidily from one phase to another, we may need to go back, for example, from abstract conceptualization to the concrete experience because we cannot draw satisfactory conclusions from reflecting on the evidence of the event itself. We need to ask more questions, check out more observations, listen to other people's perceptions and so on, before coming to a credible conclusion we would be willing to test.

Moreover, not only is the learning cycle an over-simplification of how we often learn from events, it also omits some important elements which, in practice, are crucial to the learning process. These include the relevance of emotion, one's prior expectations, the importance of memory and the nature of the learner, that is, the person who is going through the experience; these, and others, are developed further in later chapters.

LEARNING STYLES

Before leaving the Kolb cycle, mention should be made of the work carried out by Kolb in the United States, and Peter Honey and Alan Mumford[4] in the UK, into learning *styles* or *types*. Both approaches give names to the various phases of the cycle. Kolb has Diverger, Assimilator, Converger and Accommodator, whilst Honey and Mumford have Activist, Reflector, Theorist and Pragmatist. Taking the four phases of the cycle, they said that individuals may have preferences for, and particular abilities in, one or more of the phases. Developing measures for each of the phases, using a self-report questionnaire, someone can assess, for example, the extent to which he or she *senses* an experience, *reflects* on it, *generalizes* some conclusions from it, and *experiments* with those conclusions. They can then make a map of their preferences by locating their scores on the x and y axes on Figure 2.2. This produces a kite-shaped figure, Figure 2.2, which for most people is usually pulled to some extent towards one or two of the axes.

Thus the kite for someone who is very action-orientated would probably be pulled towards Active experimentation and Concrete experience at the expense of the other two phases, as in the dotted-line kite in Figure 2.2. By contrast, someone whose preference is to use each of the phases to about the same extent would have a regular-shaped kite, like a diamond (the solid line kite).

The interested reader can follow up either or both books (see the Bibliography section). However, from my point of view, both sources omit treatment or consideration of some of the elements of learning from experience which my research suggests are important.[5]

---

4   Honey and Mumford's 1986 book, *The Manual of Learning Styles*, describes their general approach, includes the self-report questionnaire and offers practical advice and guidance on how to develop any aspects of learning that are relatively weak.

5   The concept of learning styles has been criticized (see Reynolds 1997), and it must be open to question as to whether there are just four distinct and independent components relating to experiential learning. On the other hand, in my experience they have provided a useful introduction to the idea of learning from experience for people who have never previously considered it. The sequence of experiencing, reflecting, generalizing and testing intuitively feels right for most people, and the use of the styles literature helps them to dig into the overall process.

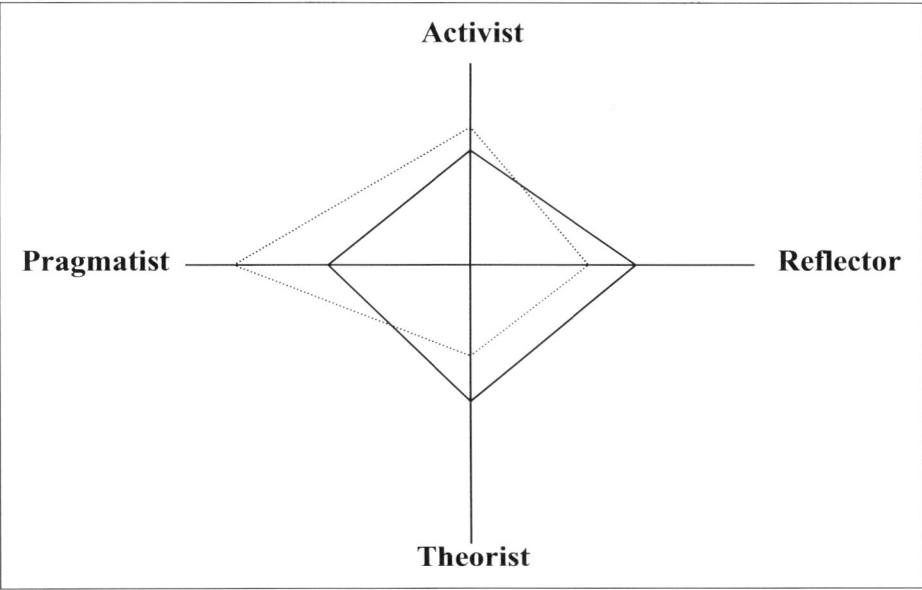

Figure 2.2   Examples of learning styles

BOUD, KEOGH AND WALKER

David Boud, Rosemary Keogh and David Walker (based in the Technology University, Sydney) focus on reflection but take a more holistic approach to learning from experience. They put forward the model illustrated in Figure 2.3.[6]

Thus in their concept of learning from experience, Boud *et al.* see a two-way process in which the experience and reflection are connected iteratively until some sort of outcome is reached. Feelings and ideas are included as part of the experience, and indeed the need to remove obstructive feelings is included as part of the reflective process. The outcomes are seen as intentions, available for future use, rather than subject to experimentation (as in Kolb).

Thus in Jim's union meeting learning experience, the *experience* of the meeting was described with graphic detail of his own and others' behaviours, and particularly his own feelings. The *reflective process* entailed going back over

---

6   Boud, Keogh and Walker contributed a chapter of their own in a book they edited entitled *Reflection: Turning Experience into Learning* (1985). The model in its complete form is on page 36 of their volume. The book contains several other interesting chapters on the general subject of reflection.

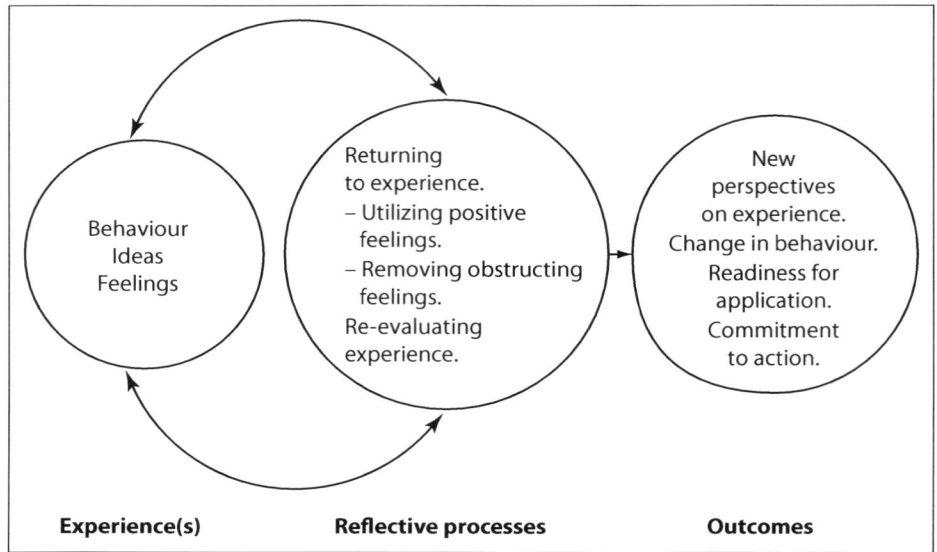

Figure 2.3   The reflection process in context

the experience, evaluating and analysing it to see where he had gone wrong, while the *outcomes* of his reflection included a determination to avoid a repeat of his embarrassment by seeking to anticipate how his words and ideas would be received.

An important point which Boud, Keogh and Walker make in their text relates to the nature of the person in relation to the experience. They say that the 'characteristics and aspirations of the learner are the most important factors in the learning process', and this is borne out by my research. My overall experience of Jim was of a man who would not avoid facing a difficulty or an unpalatable truth: someone with a different mindset could have emerged from the meeting thinking that the fault was with the union reps, and the need was for them to change. Jim faced that fact that he had failed to convince them ('everything I said they countered, and they countered it very well'), and set about rethinking his approach. In doing so, he illustrated Boud *et al.*'s outcomes of change in behaviour, readiness and commitment.

JARVIS'S LEARNING CYCLE

Peter Jarvis, at the University of Surrey, produced a learning cycle which recognizes some of the various outcomes of experiential learning.[7] He says, for example, that experiences may lead to *no learning* – because we think there is nothing new in the experience, or because we haven't the time to devote to thinking about it, or because we reject the possible conclusions from learning about it.

Jarvis also categorizes three other kinds of response to experience which do lead to learning, but which require a relatively low level of reflection. Thus we observe that something occurs, tell ourselves 'Oh, OK, so that's what happens', and move on, possibly committing it to memory, almost unconsciously. A second type of learning is that when we acquire a skill through practice and repeated drilling: many manual skills, such as using a typewriter keyboard, playing a musical instrument and learning techniques in almost all sports, are examples. A third type of learning is the mental equivalent of the second, as, for example, when we are learning things by rote, such as multiplication tables or the vocabulary of a new language.

The learning cycle which Peter Jarvis produces (Figure 2.4) takes account of these possibilities. Thus, starting with someone before an experience, The person (1), he or she may end up little different afterwards – The person (4): re-enforced but relatively unchanged. Or, following 'memorization', with greater skills or knowledge – The person (9): changed and more experienced.

Jim, learning from his poor performance in the union meeting, could be described as moving from the Experience (3) to Reasoning and reflecting (7), and Evaluation (8) immediately after the event. Thereafter, at the next meeting, using Practice and experimentation (5), he evidently found the effects of his different approach, of thinking about how his words would be interpreted, produced a better result, Evaluation (8). He committed the revised approach to memory, Memorization (6), and became a 'changed and more experienced person (9)'.

One of the attractions of Jarvis's cycle is the flexibility it allows in the treatment of an experience. Thus an experience which entails simply an observation of something, as occurs when we see someone do something with good, or bad, effects, can be remembered – memorization – and we ourselves

---

7   For a fuller account of his work see Jarvis (1994).

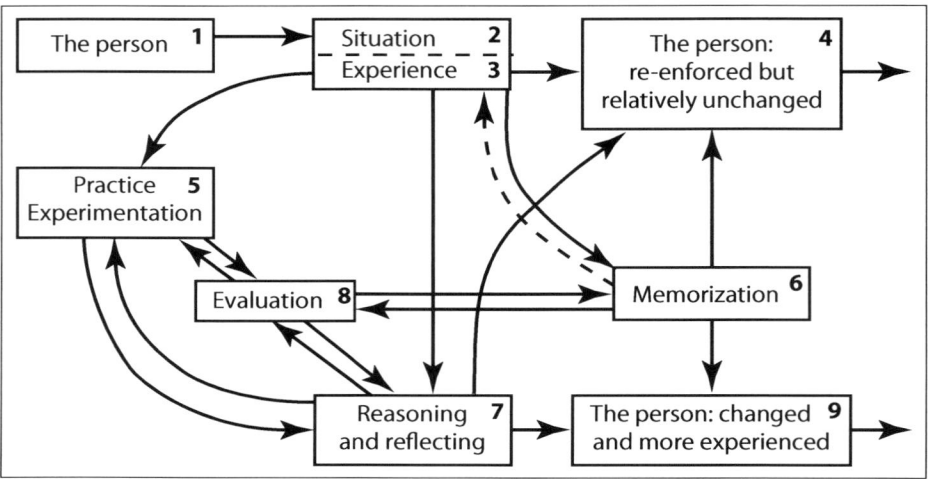

Figure 2.4   Jarvis's learning cycle

can use, or avoid, their experience in our own behaviour. A more complex experience, like Jim's, can also be tracked, as in the previous paragraph.

None of the above models of learning from experience, however, captures or encompasses all the many elements which my research colleagues illustrated, and which can come into play when we seek to make sense of something in such a way that we can use it in the future. (By *use* I mean anything from bearing it in mind, as when we recall a fact which helps to explain some other puzzle, to making a radical change in our behaviour.) As I listened in my research to people describing their experiences and how they sought to learn from them, as I read in a variety of literatures, and as I drew on my own experiences, a more comprehensive picture of experiential learning gradually evolved.[8] This is summarized in the next chapter, and developed more fully in the rest of the book.

---

8   The period of my research extended over about seven years, and a series of snapshots of the model, as it evolved over this time, is given in Chapter 15 of my thesis (Davies 2002).

CHAPTER 3

An Outline of the Model

INTRODUCTION

During my research, as I listened to my research colleagues telling me about their experiences, and as I reflected on what they said, on my own experiences and the words of writers in several relevant fields, I gradually built up a picture, a tentative model of the various elements that come into play as we convert experience into lessons, concepts, or generalized ways of behaving which we can use in the future.

Before starting to describe the Model in outline, which is illustrated in Figure 3.1, it is important to make some introductory points. The first relates to the nature of experience. In the first chapter we observed that experiences can be matters of a few moments, measured only in seconds, or they can be much longer, years even. The two examples quoted so far entailed quite short events, a few seconds for Jeannie's encounter with her bereaved friend, and minutes – less than an hour – for Jim's difficult meeting, but in each case the event was followed by quite a long period during which they thought about what happened, and sought to derive some principles from the event. For Jeannie this was the need to find a way of relating to the bereaved, while for Jim it was the need to anticipate how his message would be received. For each of them, meeting this need started immediately but continued into the future, probably for several months. Indeed, they would say that they continue to develop and refine their techniques for handling the type of situation that sparked the learning.

The nature of the experience leads to two points. First, the *learning may involve iterations between different elements* in the Model, which is why the elements are connected by two-way arrows. We can consider an event, form a hypothesis about it, but then find that it doesn't quite fit, and so go back to the event to explore it more deeply. In exploring it more deeply, we can access other sources of information and draw them into our hypothesis-making. The more complex the experience, the more puzzling and confusing it is, the more we are likely to revert back to the incident and seek more help in explaining it.

Second, the *sources of information and potential help in our understanding are variable,* depending on the experience. One type of experience would probably

entail drawing almost exclusively on, say, our own observations, as when
we taste a new food and decide whether we like it, while another type could
send us searching for explanations in books or tables, or indeed carrying out
experiments to gain greater knowledge. This latter source element I have called
'Formal knowledge'. It is in the Model because, for some types of experience, it

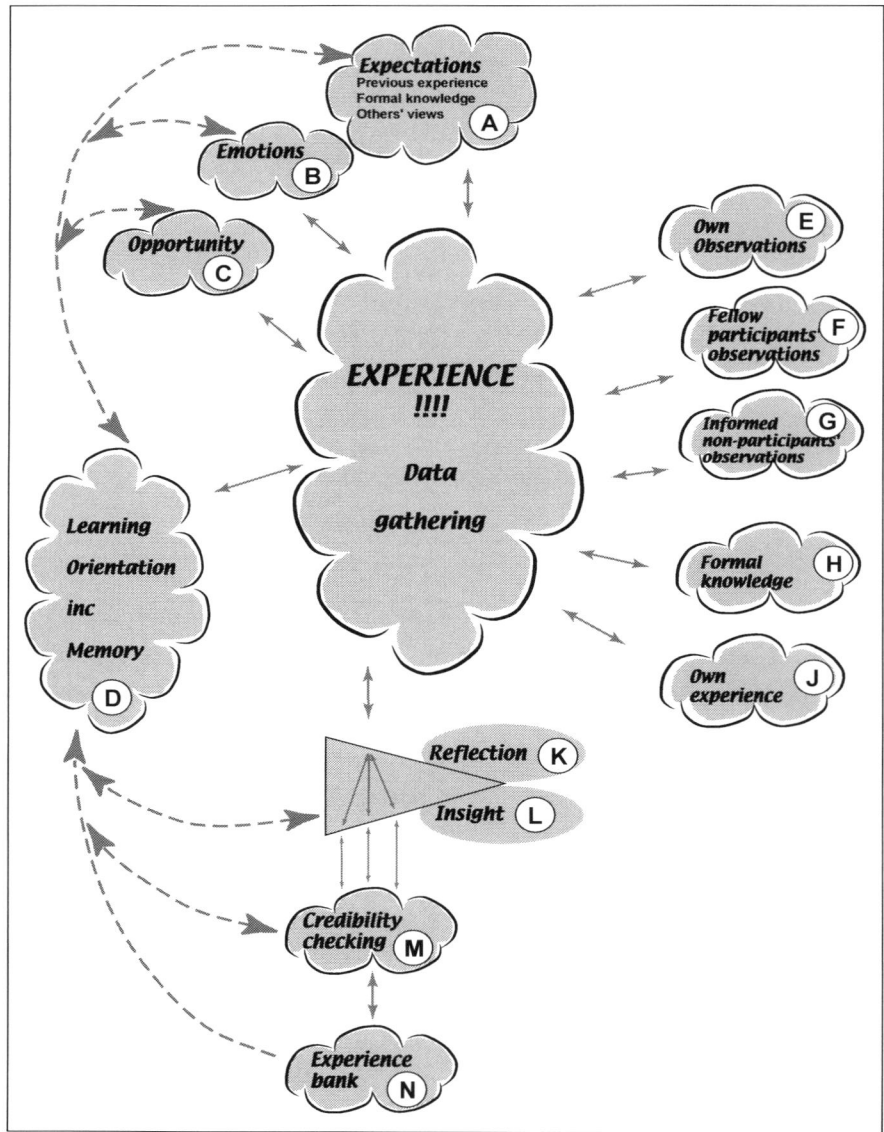

Figure 3.1   Overview of the Model of Experiential Learning

makes an essential contribution to our understanding, although for other types it may play no part. This is a general model, and it is therefore necessary to include all generic sources of help, even though in specific experiences one or more elements may not be involved.

The last introductory point is that each of the elements (with one exception) is presented in a cloud-like, fuzzy form. This is because it is generally more helpful to think of the elements as changeable, open to interpretation and reinterpretation, rather than fixed in nature. Apart from the element 'Reflection and Insight', which is shaped like a prism for reasons which will be explained later, I have avoided drawing elements in boxes, circles or other regular forms in order to remind ourselves that they are hardly ever neat and tidy, buttoned down and unlikely to change. Thus my 'Own observations' of an experience, the element which generally provides the greatest input of data, at least initially, is likely to grow and change as I think more deeply about the event I witnessed, especially as I hear other people's description of that event, or others question me about it.

WHY 'ELEMENTS'?

In the overview of the Model given in Figure 3.1, the 11 clouds, and the one prism, which cluster around the experience are referred to as 'Elements'. This word is used in the sense of an element being 'an essential part of something'. Each of the 12 elements has, or can have, a part to play in how we make sense of an experience, although, as commented in the last paragraph, the sources of data, elements E to J, tend to be specific to certain types of experience. They comprise the 'necessary and sufficient' ingredients which come into play as we move from our existence before an event comes into our reckoning to our condition after we have digested its significance and learned whatever lessons we can draw from it.

One other feature of these elements to note is that they are not similar in nature. The five on the right have some consistency in the sense that they are all potential sources of information about the experience, but the others are quite disparate. *Expectations* are concerned with what we were thinking about *before* the experience; *emotions* are triggered *by* the experience, but they are both states of mind and capable of being described at a moment in time. *Opportunity*, by contrast, is a period of time, possibly quite short, but for more complex experiences quite long.

Learning orientation, including *memory*, seeks to encapsulate for each of us as learners, our distinctive, probably unique, approach to learning. It is the one element which is relatively constant, at least in the short run, in applying to all kinds of experiences; our expectations, emotions, sources of information, and ways of reflecting may all vary according to the type of experience we encounter, but we approach them all in a way that is influenced by our particular mental make-up. I say 'relatively' constant, because, as we shall see in Chapter 7, one's learning orientation is capable of development and change over time, but in the short run it seems fairly fixed.

The elements of *reflection and insight* and *credibility checking* are different yet again, although both are the products of the interplay of nature – what we inherited, and nurture – how we developed.

So the elements are very disparate. Yet without each of them our ability to learn from a range of experiences would be reduced, and possibly impaired to the point where an experience's lessons were denied to us.

THE INFRASTRUCTURE OF REFLECTION

A dictionary definition of 'infrastructure' is 'inner structure, structure of component parts', and in this sense I use it to embrace elements A to D.

The common feature of these elements is that they provide, along with reflection, the structure of component parts of learning from experience. An approximate analogy would be with our processing of food in the digestive system: all food, no matter what kind, enters through the mouth and proceeds through the stomach, the small and large intestines, before being excreted. Depending on the type of food, this may take a short or long time, produce much, or little, of value for the body and involve some organs more than others, but they all go through the digestive system. Similarly, all experiences appear to involve the first four elements, plus reflection later on, although the type of experience is significant in influencing the extent to which each element is involved.

Expectations provide a backcloth against which to view an experience. Often, a characteristic of learning experiences is that our expectations are confounded: we expect one thing – and something quite different happens. In many cases, our expectations are in 'default mode', that is we expect, as we approach a situation, that it will be like previous situations. If, indeed, it is, and our expectations are confirmed, it is unlikely that we will learn anything new.

For example, on a regular drive to work, or the shops, if nothing occurs during the course of the drive we will probably never remember it, and learn nothing new, but if we nearly have an accident because, say, a child runs out in front of us and we have to brake sharply, that particular trip will be memorable. A learning point from it will be to be particularly aware, at that section of road,

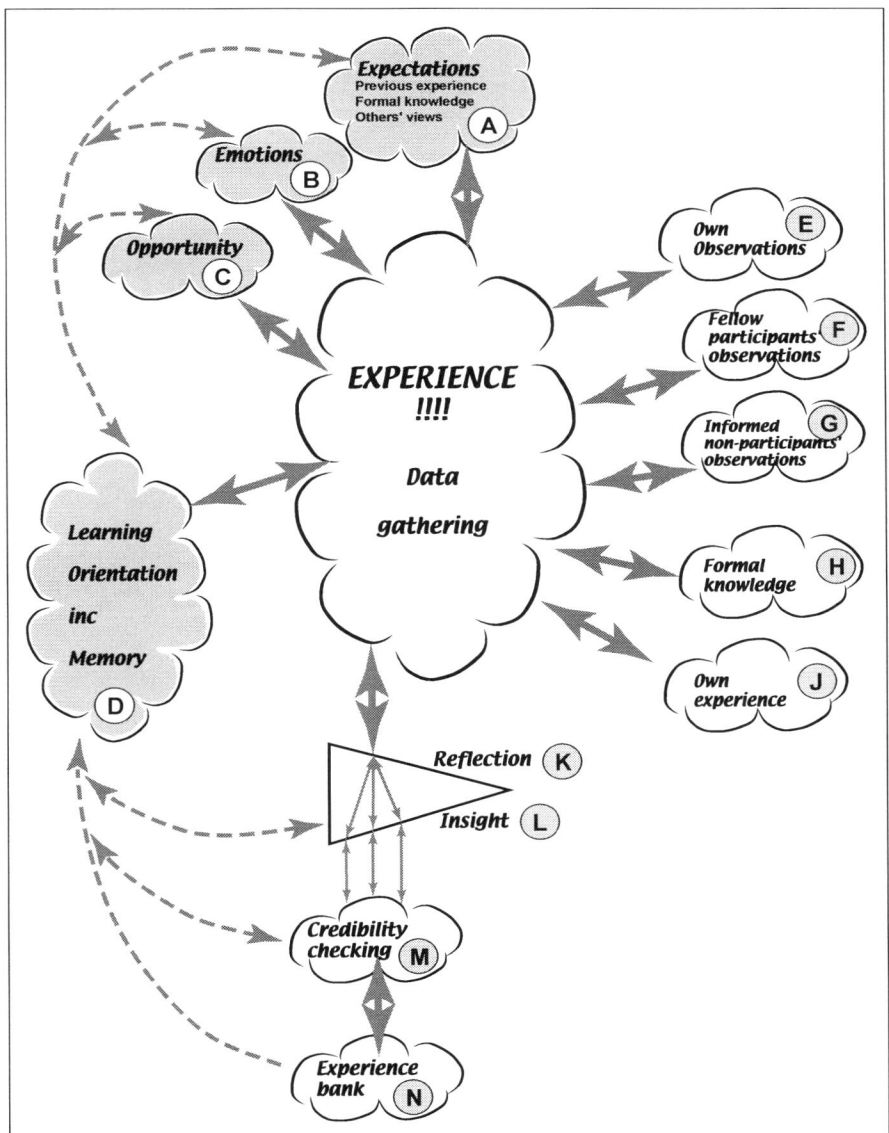

Figure 3.2   Model – the infrastructure of reflection

of the risk of an accident: our expectation of an incident-free journey will have been shattered, and we will learn to be cautious on that part of road. Chapter 4 develops these points.

Emotions are also typically associated with learning from experience. In the example above, our emotions would probably have been of fright as the child comes into our path, relief that we did not hit him or her, and anger that it should have been allowed to roam on the road. All these emotions could flood through out minds within a few seconds of the incident. On a normal run, however, which is thankfully free of such events, we feel no emotion. Or, if it is a slightly quicker run than normal, we might feel pleased and slightly curious; why is it quicker – different time of day, at the weekend, during school holidays? In this case, as our expectations are pleasantly confounded, the emotions of pleasure and curiosity lead us to analyse the causes contributing to the better performance. Chapter 5 discusses the range of emotions that may come into play when learning from experience.

The *opportunity* to reflect is an obvious component part of learning from experience, indeed so obvious that it is often overlooked. Yet a comment people sometimes make is that they have no time to learn from experience, especially if they are leading busy lives and see learning as a ponderous and taxing process. Nevertheless, if an experience has a very strong emotional content, and if it strongly contradicts our expectations, as would be the case for most people in a near-accident, the opportunity will be thrust on them. The time to reflect will be taken, possibly over and over again as the incident is relived, even if it means pushing out other thoughts. Chapter 6 analyses the nature of opportunities, and offers some suggestions for how they may be created and increased.

In the near-accident example in previous paragraphs, *most* people were said to take time to reflect, and this brings us to the last part of the infrastructure of reflection, namely our own *learning orientation*. Most people would learn from such an event, but possibly not all. It was this difference between people in their approach to learning from experience that intrigued me throughout my research. As I had observed my work colleagues as we went through some shared experience, some appeared to learn a great deal, others little and yet others virtually nothing. Of those who *did* learn, the conclusions they drew, or the lessons they learned, often varied, some learning, say, financial lessons, others technical lessons, and others organizational lessons. Why was this, when the events in the experience were common to us all?

Initially I put it down to differing mindsets, and later to different personalities, but neither of these seemed sufficient. As I thought about what my respondents had told me in our interview-discussions, and read in the fields of psychology and education, it seemed that several characteristics were brought together to form what I think of as someone's *learning orientation*, within which should be included *memory*. Learning orientation is discussed more fully in Chapter 7, but an outline follows.

'Personality' is certainly part of it. Current thinking on personality classification[1] is to identify five broad groups of traits, the 'Big Five', one of which is 'openness' to ideas and experiences. Within this broad domain there is a range, a spectrum, of types, from those who welcome the new and different, sights, sounds, tastes, touches and smells, through to those whose preference is to avoid what is new and different. It seems reasonable to suppose that people whose personality is towards the open end of this major personality grouping will be more likely to work with an experience, to seek whatever lessons it might offer, than those who prefer to avoid it. Openness is not the only contributor, however; other traits in other domains of the Big Five, such as persistence and confidence, have also been identified as contributing to learning.

However, personality on its own is insufficient to account for the nature of learning from experience. Different people, who learn a lot from a shared experience, may nevertheless learn quite different things. 'Ability', it seems, is an essential component of learning, so that ability in a particular domain enables someone to learn more from an experience than someone else who is less able. For example, someone with highly developed financial acumen or ability would be likely to learn more from a firm's bankruptcy than another person whose ability in figures and financial concepts was more basic. I argue more fully in Chapter 7 that *ability* is the product of *intelligence*, broadly defined,

---

1   See Hampson (1999) for a useful introduction to personality classification. A fundamental question is the unit of analysis: is it into whole-person types, such as Mandela-type, or Thatcher-type? Or into broad subgroup types, such as Hippocrates' cholerics or some of the more recent classifications, for example Myers-Briggs ESTJ or INFP? (Note 1 in Chapter 7 provides further references and information for Myers-Briggs.) Or is it into small units, such as traits, where a single word can describe a characteristic, such as decisive, caring, or independent?
  According to Hampson, the answer is clearly in the last category, the trait, but a problem has been the innumerable attempts by different researchers to come up with different classifications of traits. One major problem is that a trait could describe a behaviour, and/or it could explain it. The current thinking is to classify personality into a five-factor system of broad domains, called the Big Five, which Hampson says 'makes a useful structure for organising the large and confusing number of traits and their measures in vogue today' (page 285). The Big Five are: extraversion, agreeableness, conscientiousness, emotional stability and openness or intellect.

and *development*. Gardner described seven 'intelligences',[2] any one – or more, in combination – contributing in some way to the acquisition of learning from an experience, depending on how much it has been developed.

The third component in learning orientation, separate from personality and ability, is 'learned behaviour'. This is substantially independent of personality and ability, and is usually the outcome of previous experience or learning. If we have learned to review experiences, for example by becoming part of a team which routinely reflects on its performance, we are more likely to draw out some lessons than if we allow experiences to fade away. However, the practice of reviewing is one which we can pick up simply by being with others who do it automatically; it can become part of our learning orientation even though it would have been promoted by neither our personality nor our ability.

Finally, our *'memory'* plays a part in learning from experience. This is such an obvious statement that it is often overlooked, but clearly unless we are able to retain the essentials of an experience in our mind for as long as necessary, which may be months or even years, we will be unable to learn its lessons. The human mind is adept at making comparisons, and when doing so it is almost inevitable that we use our memory to compare a new experience, for example narrowly avoiding a child on the road, with earlier experiences. Memory will be discussed more fully in Chapter 8.

DATA GATHERING

The sources of information from which we draw in order to make sense of, and learn from, an experience can be surprisingly wide.

Consider the small example on the next page of one of my significant learning experiences in gardening.

The first source of information is, naturally, our *own observations*. In this example, the initial experience was what I saw, or actually did *not* see, that is a nice green sward of new grass, despite my expectations. Weeds grew on the prepared ground, but not grass, despite careful watering and covering with twigs to protect the seed from birds. Later on, in the autumn, my observation was fully up to hopes and expectations.

---

2   Howard Gardner (1993) identified the following seven separately existing and independent
     intelligences (in the order he presents them): linguistic, musical, logical–mathematical, spatial,
     bodily–kinaesthetic, intrapersonal and interpersonal.

The Grass Seed Example

I was extending the lawn by reclaiming some rough ground underneath a holly tree, and despite careful soil preparation, sowing seed at the right time during spring and subsequent watering, was disappointed by a very low germination rate – about 5 per cent of what I expected.

A gardening friend suggested that the site might be too shaded by the tree, but that didn't fit the facts, as much of the 5 per cent was actually very near the trunk. Nothing happened during the summer, and in the autumn I bought some new seed and tried again – with total success!

While pondering this change of fortune, I recalled an article I had read about the varying shelf-lives of seeds. Some seeds remain viable for many months and years, but others are very short-lived – and grass seed is in the latter category. My first sowing had been with seed which was several years old, while in the autumn it was new seed, specially bought.

My own observations were absolutely integral to learning from this event, but in many experiences we are not alone. We may be part of a team or informal group, or there may be other people around, and they will probably have their own views, literal and metaphorical, of an experience. For example, if I go to a theatre with a friend and we are particularly interested in, say, the technique of acting, it is very likely that he will point out something that I have not noticed. So the friend offers some *fellow participant's observations* which differ from my own observations. They may add to, or diverge from, my own observations, but whichever way they go they will enlarge the data I have to work on. It is a commonplace experience that two people attending the same meeting, football match, or witnessing the same road traffic incident, will have different, sometimes radically different, perspectives on what happened and why. So fellow participants' observations provide a potentially rich source of data on a shared experience.

Sometimes there are people who know about the type of experience which you have encountered, although they were not there. Their knowledge can be valuable in helping you to dig into the experience, to draw out aspects which you have not considered or to focus on issues which you have overlooked. These are the *informed non-participants' observations.* My gardening friend was performing this role, when he suggested lack of light, although his comments were actually off the mark; he had not seen the site, and if he had he would probably not have made the comment because the aspect of the site was facing due south and there was plenty of light. However, in general, shade is a problem for the growth of many plants. These three sets of observations, our own, fellow participants' and informed non-participants', are amplified in Chapter 9.

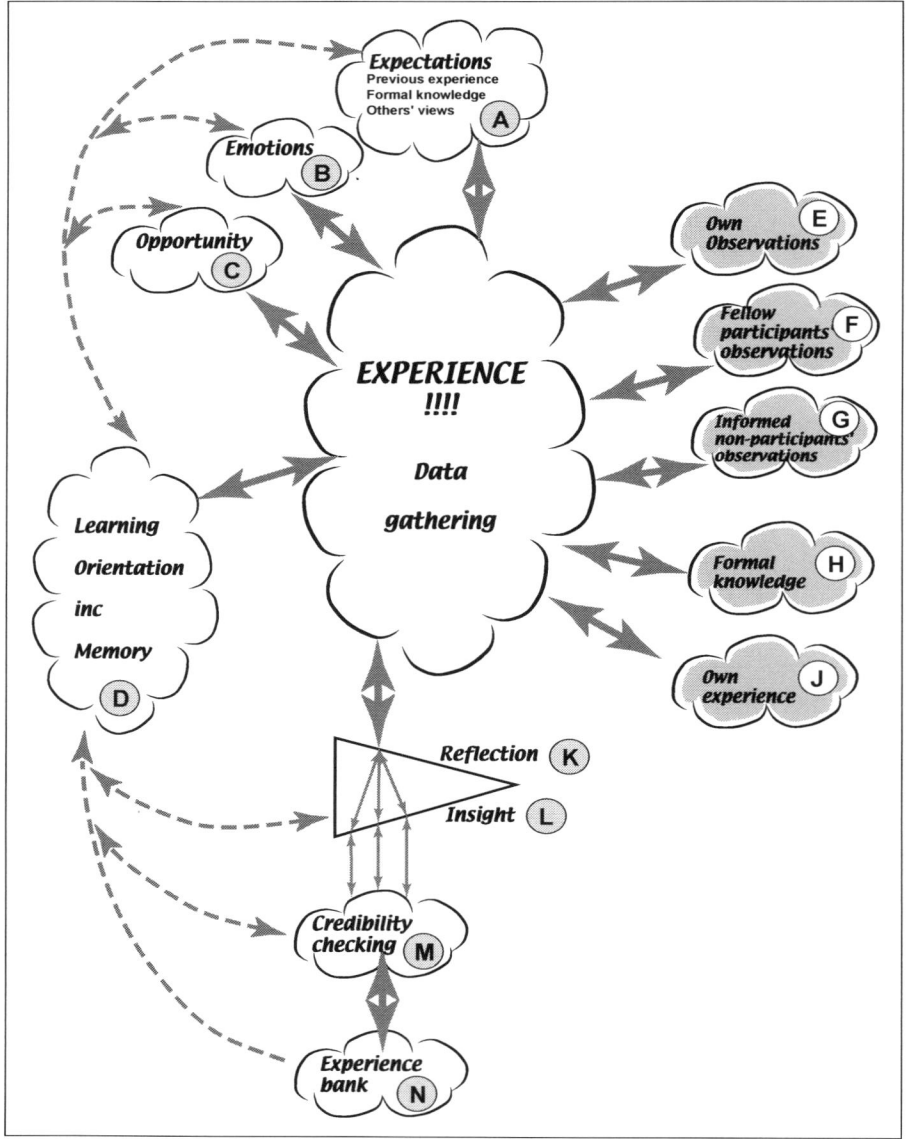

Figure 3.3   Model – data-gathering elements

(This red herring advice provides a timely warning that when learning from experience we can actually make mistakes! We can deduce lessons or beliefs which may later be shown to be plain wrong, or at best incomplete. The good news is that the broader our data-gathering base, and the more willing we are to reflect on all the evidence, the less likely will we be to fall into this trap.)

Whilst the first three elements or sources are living people with whom we have contact, the fourth is quite different. I have called this element *formal knowledge* to imply that it is in the public domain and accessible to us. The article I had read on seed germination is an example of formal knowledge, based as it was on extensive research and observations of growing from seeds.

For some types of experience this source can prove to be the most valuable, as it was for me in my gardening experience. In some domains of knowledge there is extensive literature, in the sciences, technologies and humanities, for example, which encompass this knowledge, and drawing on them – books, articles, tables – is often the key to understanding an experience. Even where the literature does not provide an immediate answer, there are techniques of research and/or experimentation which can be used to provide further data which help to explain an experience. Chapter 10 discusses formal knowledge further.

In other domains, however, there may be very little formal knowledge. This is the case for almost all our personal views of life and our fellow human beings. (Our physical lives, and to a lesser extent our mental lives, are, of course, the subject of very rich formal sources in medical textbooks and articles.) There are relatively few books which explain other people's behaviours in the quite specific circumstances we encounter in normal daily life.[3]

This brings us to the fifth element and last of these discrete sources, namely our *own experience*. As we saw earlier, from the moment of birth we have been learning from people and events around us, so that by the time we are adults we have a huge store of experience from which to draw, and which may consciously or unconsciously influence our behaviour. For example: we are walking in the street and we see someone approaching us. Assuming we don't know them, our experience of elderly people would suggest one kind of behaviour, of children on bicycles, another behaviour, of someone with a white stick, yet another and so on.

---

3   There are books on, for example, different racial, ethnic or national behaviour patterns, but these are inevitably at a high level of generalization. They are useful, however, in leading us to guard against the expectation that 'people are the same the world over'.

Chapter 10 enlarges on the use of our own past experience, but it is worth noting here that, as well as using it to inform future actions, we use it when seeking to explain anomalies when things don't happen as we expect. In my gardening example, after the first sowing I immediately covered the plot with twigs to discourage cats from scraping up the soil, and I watered it assiduously – my experience having told me that cats like a freshly raked tilth, and that seeds rarely germinate in dry soil. Both these actions were entirely appropriate, although they were insufficient to achieve success from the first sowing.

Finally, it is worth noting that we have a tendency to absorb into our own experience information and ideas that emanated from the previous three sources – *fellow participants' observations, informed non-participants' observations, and formal knowledge*, and with time to personalize them and often to forget their attributions. For example, it is well known that our own observation of, say, an argument between customers at a checkout may be enlarged by other bystanders' comments, and quite soon we will absorb those comments and present them as our own. Similarly, over time I may forget that I read an article about seed germination, and present the fact that grass seed needs to be fresh as entirely my own experience. It *is* my own experience, but in no way exclusively so. This capacity for absorption can cause problems – people can accuse you of pinching their observations, but it leads to the building up, over years, of 'own experience' into a valuable resource for sense-making and understanding new experiences.

REFLECTION AND INSIGHT AND CREDIBILITY CHECKING

Reflection and insight and credibility checking are the elements of learning from experience which all writers include to some extent in their schemas. Thus in Chapter 2, Kolb's learning cycle included the phases of reflective observation, which produced concepts, which could then be tested in active experimentation. Boud, Keogh and Walker point to several 'reflective processes', and talk about evaluating the experience, pointing to the importance of 'reality checks' which test for consistency between data. Jarvis has two-way connections between 'reasoning and reflecting' and 'evaluation' in which, once again, the outcomes of thinking about an experience are tested and possibly modified. Indeed, whole books have been written on the subject of reflection.[4]

---

4   For example, Jennifer Moon (1999) has written about reflection in the context of the development of professional skills.

In the Model, *reflection and insight* are shown as a triangle or prism, rather than in the cloud-like format for all other elements. By using the simile of the prism my intention is to suggest that a mass of data, gathered from any, possibly all, of the above five data sources, may be separated out, in the same way as a prism splits white light into its seven components, into discrete streams of

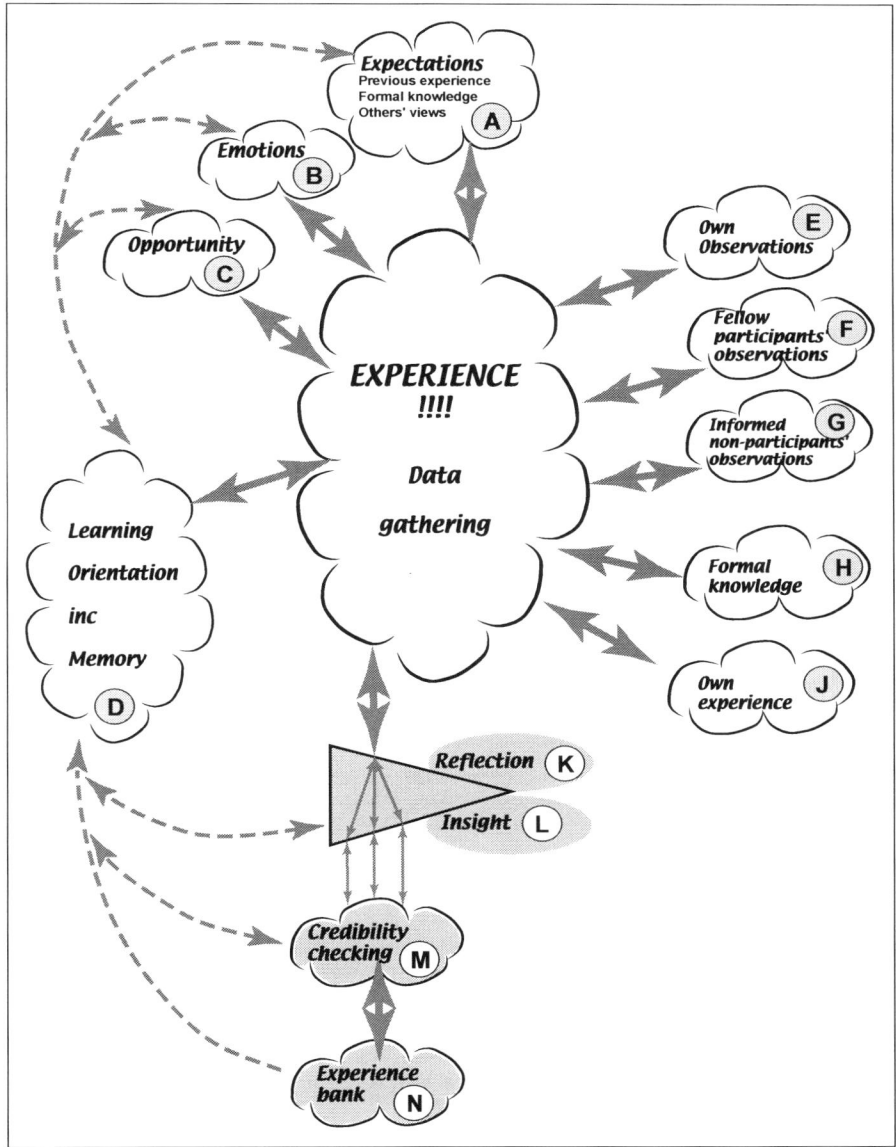

Figure 3.4   Model – reflection, insight and credibility checking

lessons from an experience. Obviously, in very simple experiences the data can be equally simple, and during reflection we can concentrate on only one set of considerations leading to one set of lessons. However, many experiences can be much more complex. For example, a colleague described how he and others had to deal with the consequences of a major burst water main, which threatened the water supply to half a city; the numerous lessons learned from that incident, which lasted over a week, came under many headings, including metallurgical, engineering, organizational, social and human relations, some becoming clear very quickly, while others took several months.[5]

Although reflection and insight are arguably different mental processes, they have been shown together because in practice it is difficult to say where one finishes and the other starts. Insights, which may sometimes come as 'Aha's!', are often preceded by a period of incubation, when the subconscious mind is mulling over the acquired data, but it would be unrealistic, and possibly artificial, to show them as separate elements. Chapter 11 develops both some of the theory in this area and offers some practical tips.

Credibility checking (discussed in Chapter 12), on the other hand, does seem to be separable, and more the product of conscious, deliberate action. I remember someone smiling ruefully as he described how he had learned from an experience, part of which included jumping to a conclusion and not subjecting it to proper scrutiny. Others described how they used homeward travel time after working on a project to check out some of the conclusions they had reached earlier in the day.

Finally, a word of warning about reflection. Someone described it to me as a 'girly thing', conveying her belief that it was an aspect of learning from experience that women are more inclined to use than men. This has not been my experience when discussing experiential learning, nor do I know of evidence which suggests that certain aspects of learning are gender specific. During my research I came across women who described themselves as very unreflective, and men who clearly spent much time pondering their experiences. It is clear to me that, if we take a version of experiential learning, say Kolb's cycle, each of the phases is important and relevant to deriving lessons from an experience, although the effort needed for any particular activity depends on the nature of the experience.

---

5   For a fuller account of this experience see Davies and Kraus (2003).

POINTS FOR EXPLORATION

Making sense of experience and learning from it is often a fairly automatic process, as when we cut a finger and learn to avoid that cutting technique in the future, but profound lessons take more thought and time. People have their own ways of accomplishing this, although they rarely seem to have much insight into these ways, so the concluding section of each of the following chapters dealing with the various elements is headed 'Points for exploration', relating to the contents of that element.

Essentially, the approach being suggested is that of asking self-directed questions designed to dig into the particular aspect of the experience. For example, recoiling from his difficult meeting, Jim would have considered his expectations of the experience, asking himself 'What did I think would happen?', 'How did I think the union reps would react?', and so on.

Answering these questions, or at least devoting a little time to pondering them, is likely to provide more information from which to make sense and learn. Many years ago, early in my career, when thinking aloud about some event or problem, I recall a colleague saying 'Well, ask yourself a question!', probably among the best five words of advice I ever had! Points for exploration offers some specific suggestions for each aspect of learning from experience.

CHAPTER 4

Expectations

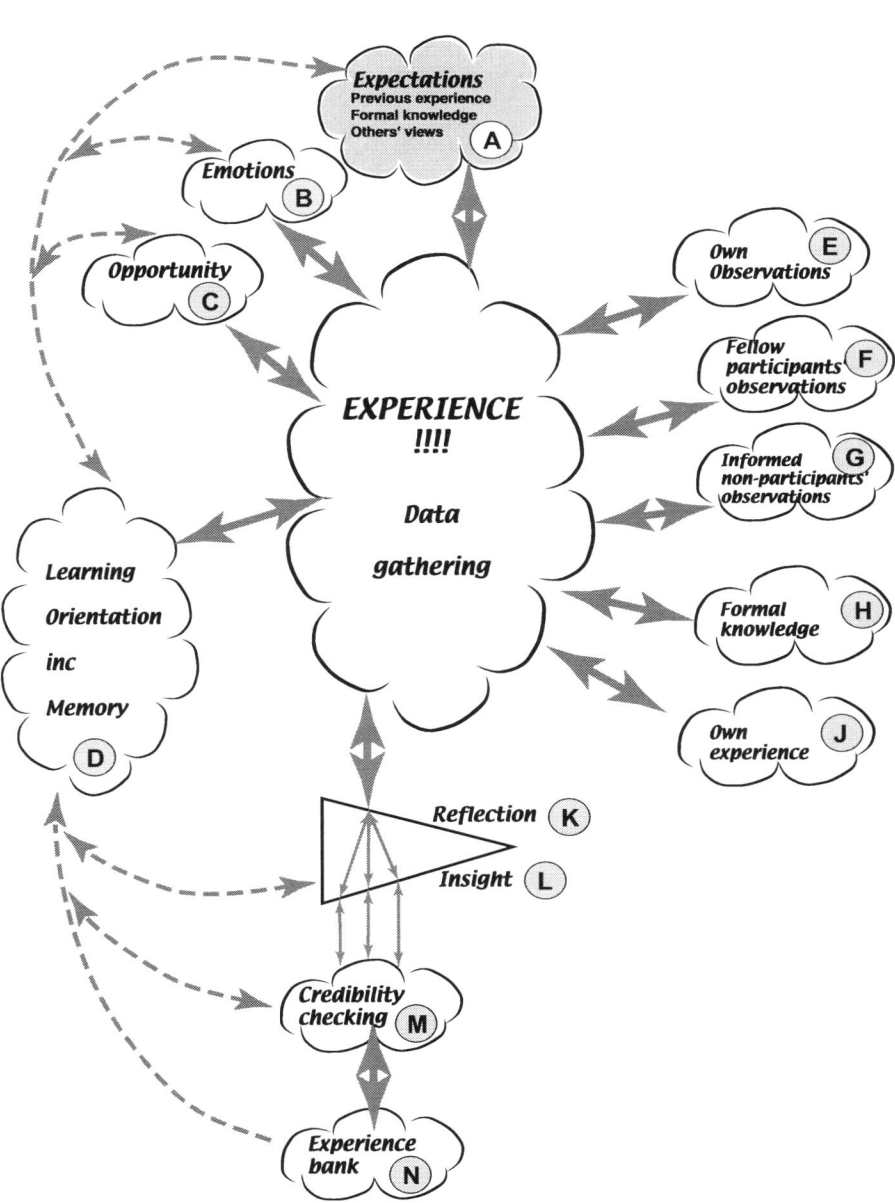

INTRODUCTION

It sounds paradoxical, but the seeds for learning from experience appear usually to be there before the experience actually occurs! The seeds are our expectations, and the learning usually occurs when those expectations are not confirmed.

By contrast, formal, taught learning – learning from books, lectures, or directly from other people, is generally a matter of acquiring some information – about a fact, a theory or a way of looking at things which we did not know beforehand, usually *confirms* expectations. Thus finding out from a reference book that the capital of Uzbekistan is Tashkent, or hearing an explanation of the difference between Darwinian and Lamarckian theories of evolution, is a kind of learning where you are absorbing what someone else has written or says, satisfies expectations. Our expectation, when opening a geographical reference book or switching on the TV for a programme on evolution, is that we will be informed on subjects where we are seeking information.

Learning from experience, however, is almost always different in that it brings about a shift in our expectations. Consider the following account:

Brearley's Discovery of Stainless Steel

Harry Brearley was a steel maker in Sheffield in the early 1900s. He was working on the metallurgy of a steel that was destined for the manufacture of rifle barrels, when he noticed that this steel seemed to be resistant to corrosion by acids and water.

This quality surprised Brearley, leading him to wonder why it was so. He was able to trace back the origin of this steel, and found that it consisted of not only iron, the basic ingredient of steel, and carbon, the usual additional element which gave steel its extra properties of strength and flexibility, but also some chromium – another metallic element which was not usually included.

Brearley realized that a steel which did not rust could be really useful, and carried out further work to discover what other properties it possessed. He was able to take out patents for these improved steels in the early 1900s, which led to the development of the stainless, or rustless, steel industry.

In this description of an actual event, the starting point of Brearley's journey of development was his recognition that something unusual had occurred, that a piece of steel had not corroded. His expectations of steel, based on years of observations on how steel behaved in different circumstances, led him to believe that when exposed to acids and water, it would begin to corrode, to rust. Yet this expectation was shattered by this particular piece of steel.

The history of science and medicine is full of such discoveries by chance, where a researcher was expecting one outcome but was surprised by another. Fleming discovering penicillin is another example. At a more personal level, each one of us makes discoveries when we expect one thing and something quite different happens.

AUTOMATIC AND CONSCIOUS THINKING

The psychologists Meryl Louis and Robert Sutton[1] distinguish between automatic thinking – 'habits of mind' – and active thinking, which they describe as the 'conscious cognitive mode'. Automatic thinking occurs when, for example, we follow a well-known routine; in Chapter 3 we talked of a regular drive to work, when in most cases our actions are conscious but automatic. We are aware of other traffic, road junctions, traffic lights and so on, but process the information they provide so automatically that afterwards we may have no recollection of the journey.

Louis and Sutton say that there is a 'sense condition for switching', that is a set of situations in which we may switch from automatic to active thinking, and they identify three ways in which this may happen. We may switch when we see something *novel*, unexpected or out of the ordinary. Thus on our journey we may see a view for the first time, because the light shines on it, or because a building which previously blocked it has been pulled down. Or 'switching is provoked by *discrepancy*', that is where something unexpected occurs. In the previous chapter an example of the unexpected was a child running into the

---

1   Louis and Sutton (1991) wrote of three kinds of situation where people are likely to focus on learning. 'First, switching to a conscious mode is provoked when one experiences a situation as unusual or *novel* – when something "stands out of the ordinary", "is unique", or when the "unfamiliar" or "previously unknown" is experienced. Second, switching is provoked by *discrepancy* – when "acts are in some way frustrated", when there is an "unexpected failure", "a disruption", "a troublesome … situation", when there is a significant difference between expectations and reality. A third condition consists of a *deliberate initiative*, usually in response to an internal or external request for an increased level of conscious attention – as when people are "asked to think" or "explicitly questioned" or when they choose to "try something new"' (page 60).

road, but it could be temporary traffic lights, or something happening inside our own car. Third, switching from automatic to active thinking can occur as a result of *deliberate initiative*, as when a previously silent passenger points out something.

In the first two types our expectations are clearly disrupted, whether by the unexpected sight of a new view, or the unexpected hazard of the child or the temporary lights. Arguably, this is also the case in the third type; our expectation is of continued silence, which is breached by the passenger's intervention.

CONSCIOUS CONTRASTS OF EXPECTATIONS

Of course, not all experiential learning starts with automatic or unconscious thinking. On many occasions we may be fully alert and aware, expecting one outcome from a situation we have thought about, only to be surprised when an entirely different outcome emerges. Brearley, working on the physical strength of gun barrels, was surprised to see that the metal he was testing wasn't corroding. His 'default mode' of expectation concerned the physical strength of the steel, but the alloy steel attracted his attention because, unlike all other steels in his extensive experience, it did not corrode.

Many of the accounts of learning from experience which I have heard have started with descriptions of what people expected or assumed would happen, closely followed by what actually did happen. Some accounts were of pleasurable surprises, as when Al described how a team he was leading to tackle a severe crisis worked so well that they actually thought of their work as fun! Others were the complete opposite; I heard a harrowing account of how, following the takeover of his firm, Rick, a financial expert, was systematically forced out of his employment. His expectation, based on his career to date of ten successful years, was that working hard and producing good results guaranteed the esteem of his employers, yet despite this he found himself being threatened – and the harder he worked, the more he was threatened. He was thinking 'What have I done wrong?', when in fact he had done nothing wrong; he was the victim of a particularly Machiavellian takeover process where the most senior people are sacrificed. His learning from that experience was that 'the world can be a cruel place, and you have to look out for yourself'. Yet others were fairly neutral, as in the discovery of stainless steel described above.

In the Model, the expectations cloud also contains the words *Previous experience, Formal knowledge,* and *Others' views*. These are the principal sources of our expectations. Most of our day-to-day learning from experience arises when the expectations based on our own previous experience are confounded; for example, when someone we had previously thought of as perennially good-natured shows a callous and cruel side of their character, or when someone we think of as having little to offer comes up with a really helpful suggestion. Discrepancies, to use Louis and Sutton's word, in formal knowledge are often the starting point of advances in science and engineering, and are probably less common in everyday life, although they can be very powerful. Many years ago when using compass to navigate in the Lake District I found my results were strange and defying common sense; later I read that the area where this had occurred, Crinkle Crags above the Langdale Valley, had magnetic rocks which could cause compass deviations. Others' views often colour our expectations, when, for example, a friend tells us we will enjoy a film, or that another person is an unreliable colleague: our judgement of the film or the colleague will be influenced by the expectation created, and will probably be the more memorable if it is confounded. In this case, we will probably also seek to find out why our friend held their views.

INTERACTION OF SITUATION AND INDIVIDUAL

It is obvious that expectations are very personal, depending on our previous experiences and background. Even identical twins, brought up in the same environment, have slightly different perspectives, and their expectations will accordingly differ. Most people handling Brearley's gun barrels, or seeing Fleming's petri dish of penicillin mould, would not have been struck by the contrast between what they expected and what actually happened, and thus would not have been moved to follow up as did those two researchers. (Even if they did notice the discrepancies, they still may not have pursued them; Chapter 7 on *learning orientation* will consider why some people follow up anomalies and others do not.) In general, people with expertise in a given field are more sensitive to, and have more precise expectations of, a particular situation than someone who is a novice in that field. Consequently, the expert is more likely than the novice to see discrepancies when they occur.

POINTS FOR EXPLORATION

We said at the start of this chapter that expectations are the seeds of learning from experience, so it makes good sense when trying to learn from a particular experience to ask ourselves some questions along the following lines:

- What were our expectations beforehand? Were they that there would be no change from previous similar events? Or were we expecting one set of outcomes, but actually observed quite different ones?

- Why did we have those particular expectations? What was there in our past that led us, through our own experience, through formal knowledge, or others' views, to have those expectations.

- What is novel or discrepant about the experience, or has prompted us to consider it?

- How would our expectations change in the light of the experience?

It is also a good idea to practise these questions by starting with an experience you have had in the past from which you learned some, or even one, important lessons. Think of an incident when you were quite surprised by what happened, and your view of things, or people, changed significantly. Doing this, you will have started on reflective thinking!

CHAPTER 5

Emotions

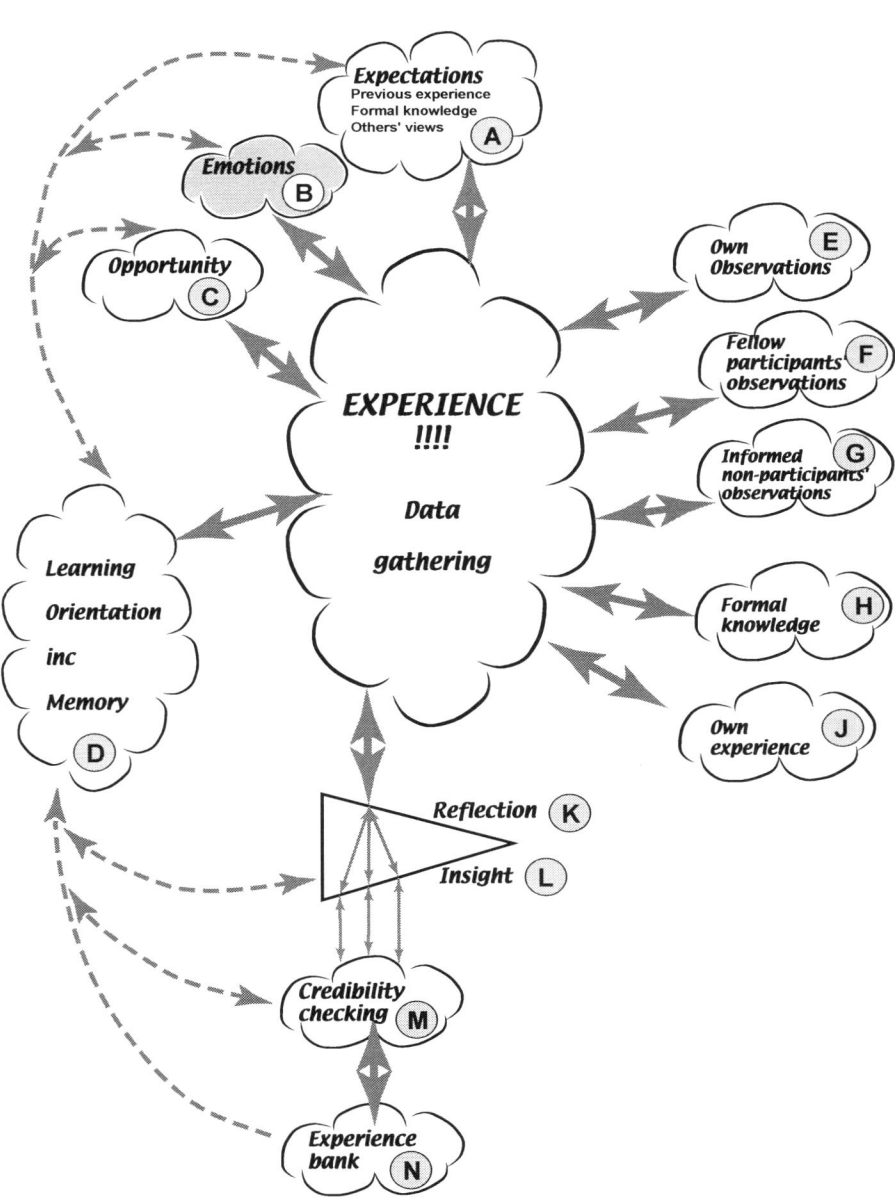

Expectations
Previous experience
Formal knowledge
Others' views
(A)

Emotions
(B)

Opportunity
(C)

Own Observations
(E)

Fellow participants' observations
(F)

Informed non-participants' observations
(G)

EXPERIENCE !!!!
Data gathering

Learning Orientation inc Memory
(D)

Formal knowledge
(H)

Own experience
(J)

Reflection (K)
Insight (L)

Credibility checking (M)

Experience bank (N)

INTRODUCTION

Very early in my exploration of how people learn from experience I noticed that emotions played a significant part in starting the process. This realization came both from a study of the words that were used, which conveyed, sometimes quite vividly something of the state of the speaker's arousal, and also from the body language which accompanied their accounts. Consider the short examples of learning given in earlier chapters. In the example in Chapter 1 Jeannie felt ashamed, felt that she had let down her friend, her colleagues and herself. In his meeting, Jim, in Chapter 2, felt he was 'a gibbering idiot', and thought 'never again, I'll never again allow myself to get into this situation'. As they spoke, their postures leaning forward, the quality of their voices and their general demeanour of people who had had painful experiences, conveyed the importance they attached to these learning events in their lives.

For other events, emotions of pleasure and joy accompanied descriptions of learning. Al, for example, described his great satisfaction and pleasure at leading a team charged with tackling a crisis; he said 'We had as much fun as you can have with your clothes on!' Tim evoked a more cerebral pleasure when he realized the power of being able to practise systems thinking, that is seeing an organization, or a major area of it, as a whole, composed of separate but interconnected parts, and being able to see how one part impacted on another. Al's and Tim's animation when describing these experiences was indeed memorable.

A third type of emotion, less manifest but undoubtedly there, came in the cluster of curiosity – surprise, wonder, and puzzlement.[1] Harry Brearley's emotion, in Chapter 4 was one of surprise and puzzlement that something he had expected to happen, namely that steel would corrode, had not occurred. Similarly, my own emotions in the grass seed example in Chapter 3 were those of curiosity, tinged with annoyance, that despite careful preparation, my patch of lawn seed had not grown.

So in the development of the model of learning from experience, an element entitled *emotions* was incorporated very early on, and the purpose of this chapter is to explore the contribution emotions make to our learning, the ways in which they do it, and some limitations to their impact.

---

1   Not all psychologists include the surprise/wonder/curiosity cluster as true emotions. Clore (1994), for example, suggests that 'they are not emotional feelings, but what might be called "cognitive feelings" or feedbacks on our state of knowledge'. However, this seems a fine distinction, and I will go with the majority who include them. For a comprehensive classification of emotions see Averill (1997).

THE PURPOSE OF EMOTIONS

The psychologist Gerald Clore (1994) says[2] that 'a primary function of emotion is to provide information'. Through our facial expressions and body language we convey information to other people; so if, for example, we appear to be suddenly terrified, other people will look to find the reason why – because perhaps they too should be terrified, and take action accordingly. Of greater relevance to our learning from experience, however, Clore writes that 'emotions supply information … to oneself through distinctive thoughts and feelings'. So in the examples above, the information supplied to both Jim and Jeannie, the feelings of inadequacy and shame, prompted a profound wish to avoid that type of embarrassment in the future by preparing themselves appropriately. For Al and Tim the information was quite different: their feelings of pleasure and satisfaction pointed up their belief that what they had learned was good, helpful, and should be of use in the future. The emotions of surprise and curiosity which Harry Brearley felt in his non-corroding steel example, and I in my grass seed puzzle, prompted us into exploring the reasons for our observations, and using the outcomes to learn more.

In this sense, emotions complement *expectations* in kick-starting the learning process. An event or experience which has not challenged our expectations, and to which we have passive feelings, that is, no raised emotion, is very unlikely to receive any further attention, and as such will not be used as the basis for learning. As children, many things are new, different, exciting (or awful), and so we learn extensively from them, but as adults, particularly when working in a familiar environment on relatively routine activities, the opportunities for learning are far fewer. For much of our time we are, in Louis and Sutton's terms, in automatic thinking mode. This is, of course, energy efficient, because dealing with new, different and potentially perplexing situations requires more effort, that is, it takes more energy, than when running along in a familiar manner.

Not only do emotions provide information, which may jolt us out of our coasting behaviour, they can also cause us to prioritize. Clore goes on[3] 'Emotions guide one's attention to things that are relevant to goals and concerns that are implicated in the emotional situation … Such processes ensure that what appears most relevant is attended to first.' For example, if we suspect that there is a fire in the next room, our fear for our lives, and those of others, will impel us to stop whatever we are doing and check whether our suspicions are justified, and if so to take immediate action. The fear of death, the strongest

---

2   Clore (1994), page 103.
3   Clore (1994), page 105.

of all emotions, forces out all other plans and intentions until such time as the cause of the fear has been removed. This is a basic survival instinct: someone who is unable to feel fear would be unlikely to survive. (Someone who is a trained firefighter would retain their fear of fire, although familiarity with it, and the knowledge of how to tackle it, make them able to act more confidently than someone with less experience.)

The strong emotions associated with a learning experience also have the effect of making the event, and the learning that comes from it, very memorable. When I was listening to people describe their learning experiences they were often relating events that had occurred many years earlier, sometimes several decades before. Nairn, for example, described with obvious pleasure and satisfaction, how – 35 years earlier! – he had learned a particular technique when, as a young engineer running a challenging project on his own, he was faced with and overcame a technical problem well outside his textbooks. Rick, the financial expert mentioned in the chapter on expectations, was describing a significant event which had happened over 20 years earlier.

So it appears that emotions make events memorable. It is not so much the nature of the emotion, whether it is of pleasure or pain or surprise, as its strength that decides its memorability. It seems we are more likely to remember experiences marked by really strong emotions, and to remember the lessons that we derive from those experiences.

Experiences which bring less strong emotions, however, may be forgotten along with their emotions, but their *lessons* nevertheless remain with us. A colleague, Dan, and I once were involved in a very heated meeting with our boss, following which Dan made some particularly perceptive observations on the dynamics of the meeting. Years later I could recall very clearly the whole of the meeting and Dan's subsequent comments, but when I mentioned it to him Dan had totally forgotten the event. Its emotional charge for me was much greater than for Dan, probably because I was perhaps lucky to keep my job! Yet I know that Dan remembered the lessons he had learned from it because I saw him put them into practice later in comparable situations.

It hardly needs adding that emotions do not serve their purpose if they are wallowed in or otherwise indulged. Their purpose is to draw to our attention matters which may have importance or significance, and having done that our brains can then address the issues they have raised. If we spend time bemoaning our fate, or otherwise remaining in the condition of exploring our feelings at length, we are putting off the creative stages of considering what we can learn and what we can do as a result of the experience. Jeannie and Jim, in responding to their quite profoundly disturbing events, provide good examples of how emotions can then be focused on interpreting what had happened, and taking action to prepare themselves for future similar occurrences. Within a very few hours they were leaving the emotion phase and thinking about what could be done to equip themselves for later similar situations.

Finally, in this section on the purpose of emotions, it is worth noting that our emotions are sometimes more fundamental than our ability to express them. People vary enormously in their capacity to describe emotions; some have extensive vocabularies, drawing on words with subtly different shades and nuances of meanings, and for them the choice of words to convey an emotional reaction may be relatively easy, while others, lacking that facility in language, expression may be difficult. It is well known that, for everyone, language is full of pitfalls.[4] Even the most self-aware and verbally dextrous person will come upon an experience which is so new, different and compelling, and whose emotional charge so distinctive, that their immediate ability to put it into words is inadequate, and yet the message conveyed by the emotion could be crucial to survival, or have other lasting significance. We ignore our emotions at our peril.

EMOTIONS: A HEALTH WARNING

While there is no doubt that emotions are valuable in drawing our attention to events and occurrences which are important to us, there is anecdotal and experimental evidence that those same emotions tend to cloud our judgement. Gerald Clore, for example, quotes experiments where students responded to interviews about their satisfaction with their lives on days when the weather was either cold and rainy or warm and sunny.[5] Respondents were happier on warm, sunny days than when it was cold and rainy, and they judged their lives more satisfactory. Interestingly, however, when the interviewer drew attention to the weather, the students appeared to discount it when making judgements on their life-satisfaction. This is a significant observation to which we will return in Chapter 9 when we examine the contribution to experiential learning which can be made by *informed non-participants*.

---

4   Writers on language discuss the problems of using words to convey meanings. The American linguist Chomsky, for example, points to the way people, particularly in childhood, build up an ability to express themselves, and to understand totally new concepts. The French philosopher Derrida shows how, by deconstructing a text, a writer has made assumptions, and incorporated ambiguities, often without being aware of what they were doing.

5   Clore (1994), page 106.

Clore also suggests that different emotions lead to different ways of thinking about experiences, that is different ways of learning from them.[6] When people feel positive emotions they are more likely to think outwards, to expand the ways of looking at the experience, use other models and analogies and take different perspectives. When they feel negative emotions, however, they tend to draw down into the experience, to focus on details, being systematic, analytical and controlled. Although the evidence on this particular subject was relatively sparse when Clore was writing, an analysis of my colleagues' learning from their experiences tends to confirm this distinction between positive and negative emotion. As an example of positive emotion, Tim, learning from experience of the techniques of systems thinking could readily envisage ways in which it could be used in the understanding of a wide range of activities, from the organization of a chemical works to the running of a sports club, or the dynamics of his own family. Jim, on the other hand, filled with negative emotions following his awful meeting, focused very inwardly on what had gone wrong, how he had performed so badly, and in great detail on what he needed to do to achieve a better result next time. Interestingly, his subsequent experience was very positive; he had learned the technique of preparing what he said by anticipating how it would be received by his listeners, who, in the first instance, were his union colleagues at the resumed meeting. This technique worked very well, and as Jim described it to me his emotions changed from negative (shame, despair) to positive (satisfaction, even pleasure), and he described how this technique applied to all types of audience, including customers, suppliers, peer colleagues and the community. In this positive emotional frame he was manifestly expanding outwards, exploring new opportunities for using a new technique.

Another situation where emotions do not lead, at least for some time, to the creative stages of learning is where the emotional charge is so strong that it blots out the possibility of purposeful thinking. Examples include the death of someone very close to us, or the witnessing of some cataclysmic event beyond our imagination. In both these situations it is as though the body shuts down the creative, cognitive parts of our being in relation to the event in question, although not to other aspects of living – such as housework, travelling, or routine work, until such time as we can mentally accommodate the new circumstances. In these cases it is best to 'listen to our body', and not seek to move from the emotion phase too early.

---

6   Clore (1994), pages 109–110.

POINTS FOR EXPLORATION

It would be a useful first step to test the notion that emotions provide information. So some reflections on our own experiences may be helpful:

- Think of one or two fairly recent experiences – good or bad, positive or negative – and identify the emotions associated with them.

- What lessons did you learn from these experiences? For example, knowing more about a customer's background before asking how our product was received; planning a meal by anticipating the times needed for preparing each part of each course; making allowances for roadworks when setting off on a long car journey.

- Don't neglect good experiences, such as successes and triumphs, where your emotions were of pleasure and satisfaction. What was it about these good experiences that contributed to positive emotions? How did they come about, and how can they be replicated in the future?

CHAPTER 6

Opportunity

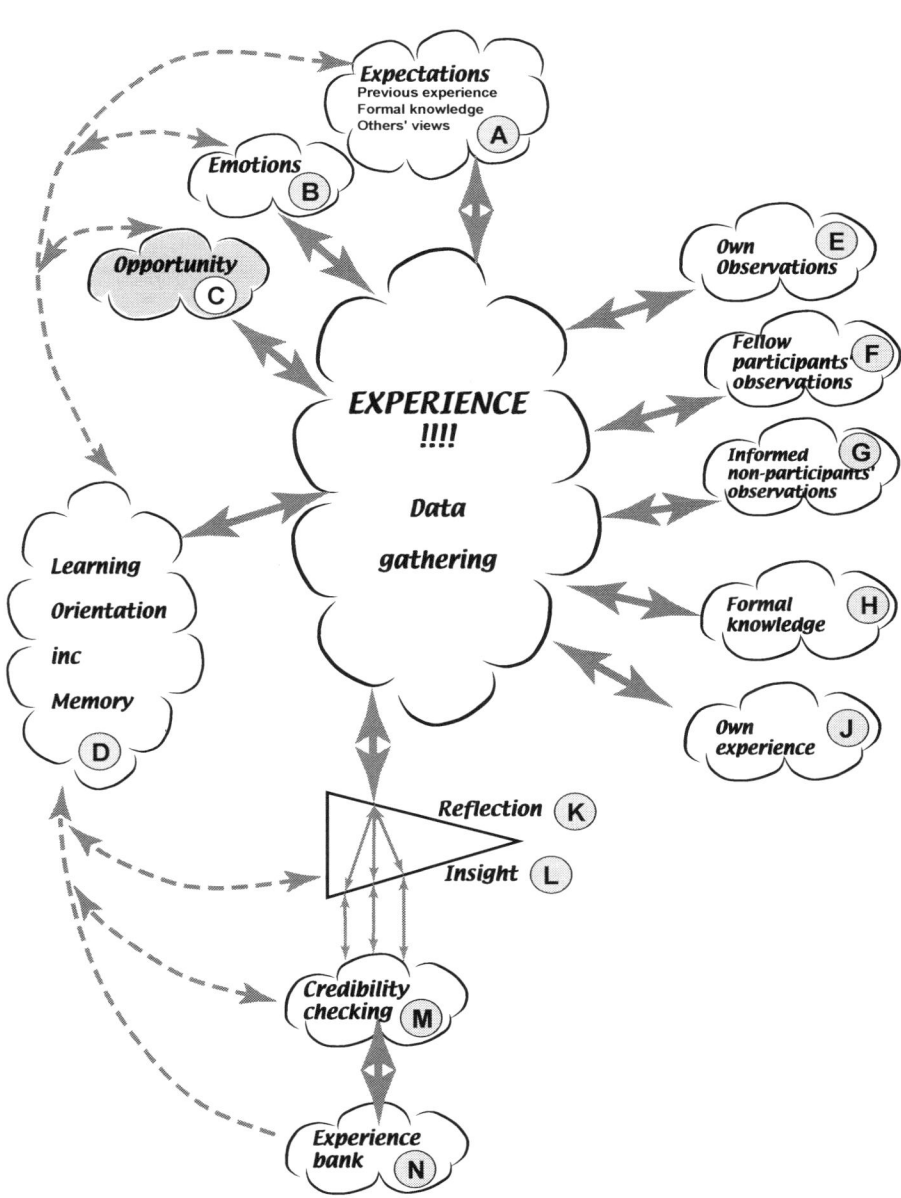

INTRODUCTION

By contrast with *expectations and emotions*, the need for *time* to consider an experience, to reflect upon it and seek whatever insights it offers, was one of the last of the elements in the Model to be incorporated. It did not exist in the penultimate version which I was discussing with Sam, a friend who runs a busy training organization, when she said, gesturing to the Model with its many clouds and arrows, 'Of course, most people would never have the time needed for all this!' She had a point, and she compelled me to go back to all the interviews I had had with people who clearly *had* made time to consider their experiences, and to wonder why they had managed to find the time in their busy lives to come to conclusions which had great significance for them. (Interestingly, Sam herself illustrated one way in which busy people *make* time, as we shall see later in this chapter.)

Part of the answer probably lay in the previous two elements, expectations and emotions, because severely shaken expectations and strongly aroused emotions would thrust the experience to the top of one's consciousness. In this way they would be like physical experiences, cutting or burning oneself, or other traumatic experiences like the near-accident with the child in Chapter 3. The sheer strength of the experience compels both attention and the desire to learn – generally what *not* to do in the future. For these kinds of experience, opportunity is not optional; it is compulsory.

Another part of the answer probably lies in the nature of the person who experiences the event. We will look at this in more detail in the next chapter, but it is sufficient to say here that some *learning orientations* are more likely to dwell on, and seek to learn from, an experience than others. The tendency towards reflective observation, one of the phases of experiential learning we met in Kolb's cycle, shown in Figure 2.1 (page 12), varies enormously between people, as anyone who has seen the 'kite shapes' (Figure 2.2, page 15) completed using the Honey and Mumford (1986) questionnaires will testify. Reflective observation and abstract conceptualization are phases which may require time and effort, and people vary in their willingness to provide opportunities for them.

A SPECTRUM OF OPPORTUNITIES

Before looking at how opportunities can be created and used for learning from an experience, it may be helpful to observe that there is a gradation of criteria for deciding whether to dwell on an experience and derive whatever lessons it offers. At one extreme are the physical, and sometimes mental, events which compel us to pay attention in order to avoid similar suffering in the future. For example, if we pick up broken glass and inadvertently cut ourselves, we will try a different method of picking up broken glass the next time we have to do it – for example, by using a brush and dustpan. For both Jeannie and Jim, in their bad experiences, their senses of inadequacy and shame were sufficiently strong to force them to find different ways of behaving. These could be labelled *self-compelled* opportunities.

An intermediate category could be called *directed* opportunities. These are less compelling than the above but are nevertheless followed because in the past we have learned of their value, or perhaps someone has required us to make an opportunity. Thus many jobs require us to *review*, as part of normal process, what has happened, especially when we are consciously setting out to learn from an event. For example, military training manoeuvres, training sessions for student teachers delivering lessons for the first time, and trainee chefs planning and preparing, say, a lunch party, are all followed after the events by de-briefing or review sessions as a formal part of the learning process. The aim of the review is to consider what happened, what went well (but might nevertheless be improved), what went less well, or even badly, and thus requires attention before the manoeuvre, lesson or lunch is tackled next time. Learning logs are often an integral part of this process; part of their value is that by writing down what happened very shortly after the event, one is forced to think about it in some depth, and thus to look for the learning points which emerge from the review.

In the public world, inquests and courts of enquiry are examples of directed opportunities for reviewing what has happened. Thus in an inquest, the coroner is charged with finding out the causes of someone's death, so that if, for example, they are suspicious, the police can be called upon to investigate further, or if there has been a plane crash a court of enquiry can find the causes.

At the other end of the spectrum are the genuinely *discretionary* opportunities, where neither the gravity of the experience, nor any external or learned discipline, compels us to take time to reflect, but nevertheless on an individual basis we can try to find out why something happened. These are discretionary in the sense that no one outside is telling us how to do it, or even whether to do it at all. Consequently, we may, or we may not, make the opportunity to consider an experience in this category, and our first decision, therefore, is influenced by the extent to which we think it is worthwhile putting effort into this consideration.

The majority of the examples of learning from experience which people shared with me during my research were of this last type, where they had made an opportunity, and put effort into it. One of my regrets when looking back on our discussions is that I did not explore with them how they made time for considering these types of experience, or whether they had a preferred way of approaching them. However, by looking back on the interview transcripts, by drawing on my own experiences of myself and others, and by reference to a few books, the following paragraphs address the questions: how can we make opportunities for learning from experience? and, given an opportunity, what could we do?

MAKING OPPORTUNITIES

Opportunities require time, so we are in the realm of time management. It is a truism that 'experts have time', that is to say, when they are using their expertise they have more time for considering what they are doing than would beginners or amateurs in similar situations. Extreme examples would include professional footballers who, even when the game is carried on at a furious pace, have time to read what is happening and to turn events to their advantage. Similarly, performing musicians are able to reflect on how they are sounding and take decisions on tempo and dynamics, when amateurs are simply hoping to finish in reasonable order. The educationalist Donald Schön[1] has referred to this process as 'reflection-in-action', although his principal examples are of more deliberate reflection – an architect working with a difficult site, and a coaching psychotherapist working with a trainee psychotherapist.

In these cases, the review process is part of an automatic feedback loop, albeit conducted at different speeds, in which the person carrying out the action, sometimes referred to as the actor, is considering both what has happened and the implications for the future as he or she is proceeding. For them, the opportunity to reflect is built into the process. However, for many experiences, the opportunity to reflect only really occurs at the end, after the event, and it is this kind of opportunity that this section is looking at.

Here are some examples where people have created opportunities to consider events which have recently passed:

1   Donald Schön (1983) wrote about how professionals think in action in his book *The Reflective Practitioner*.

- Driving home following training sessions she had been conducting. Interestingly, this was given by Sam who, as mentioned at the beginning of this chapter, said that busy people would not have time for reflection!

- Flying back from a meeting with customers. Alan, a finance expert based in Wall Street, said 'Be obsessive about looking backwards as much as looking forwards … This is not a disciplined process; I have a "separate brain" for this in which my eyes look backwards! I find that thoughts suddenly jump out of my head.'

- Dan, a colleague whose overall behaviour conveyed great skill in learning from experience, always followed an important monthly meeting with a visit to the barber! There, in peace and quiet, he was able to ponder the events of the meeting, following which he would return to his office and take appropriate action.

- Meeting a buddy: Jim, later in our discussion in which he described his awful meeting, talked of the value of meeting a particularly perceptive colleague to chat over events. In his case it was in a pub after work, but other people mentioned using coffee breaks, meals, walks and even the gym as opportunities for reviewing the events of the day. The colleague need not have been involved in Jim's experience, but he knew the organization, its background, and the issues it was facing. (We will look in more detail at the value of working with other people in Chapter 9.)

- Revisiting with colleagues: the above four examples primarily entailed reflections on an experience, but informal learning can involve much more. Going back over an experience with colleagues who were there, whether it be in the car park after work, over coffee or lunch, or in a formal review session, can be invaluable in refreshing your own memory and/or new perceptions and data. Al, leading a team through a period of crisis, found team time spent recapping, before reflecting, invaluable.

- Keeping notes: many people find the discipline of writing notes or learning logs tedious, but those who do always attest to their value. Gary made summary notes on his overseas work, and referred extensively to them during our discussions. Notes have two distinct advantages:

(i)   the very act of writing something down helps to formulate it in one's mind, even, or perhaps especially, if what you write is mainly about questions or unresolved issues; and

(ii)   going back to them after a short period, say only three or four days, is helpful in jogging the memory and reviving significant details.

The trick with notes is not to make them too formal. Phrases rather than sentences, short sentences rather than long, the use of exclamation marks to identify issues, and question marks to identify puzzles – all these help to jot down in a strictly personal way the things that strike you about an event or experience. Mind maps could be particularly helpful: their great value is that, by using the whole of a sheet of paper, they enable one to capture several quite disparate observations or thoughts very quickly, and in such a way as to enable them to be developed. Their principal exponent is Tony Buzan.[2] (There is more on the value of writing in Chapter 9.)

•   Planning opportunities: busy people often use their diaries to reserve time for preparation before important events or meetings, for example to write papers or think about how a meeting should be conducted. Similarly, space could be reserved after the event/ meeting to consider what has happened; this is often used for follow-up action, and it could be extended for a few minutes for pondering less clear issues. One of my 'best bosses' clearly allotted time after meetings for reflection and follow-up action.

•   Thinking in bed! One person mentioned the value of reviewing the events of the day before she went to sleep. It was as though, having brought them into focus, she could then park them for the time being and get her rest. The real bonus for her was that, very often, difficult issues seemed a lot clearer the next morning. (The section on eurekas in Chapter 11 on reflection and insight discusses some of the underlying reasons why this can be so.)

These are a few examples of ways of making opportunities for learning from experiences. You could probably think of more! The important thing is to work out what works best for you, and experiment and develop it.

---

2   Tony Buzan has written several books on mind maps, e.g. *The Ultimate Book of Mind Maps* (2005).

USING OPPORTUNITIES

The question now arises: what do I do when using an opportunity? If I have, say, reserved half an hour in my diary after an important meeting, or decided to use the travelling time home after an event, how do I use that time?

Essentially, it is an occasion for considering what has happened. The word often used is reflection, although for some people this implies a rather passive approach. Several near-synonyms are: making sense, pondering, analysing, mulling over and even wondering.

The detail of the answer obviously depends on the nature of the meeting or event, and how you viewed it. In general, whether it was a success or a disaster, the questions are: *Why* was this so? *What* led to it being something to replicate in the future, or avoid at all costs? *What* is there to bear in mind for future meetings or events? *How* would I apply whatever lessons emerge from it?

Note that these are *open* questions, designed to elicit as much information as possible. The Victorian writer Rudyard Kipling summed it up in his poem *The Elephant's Child*:

> *I keep six honest serving-men*
> *(They taught me all I knew);*
> *Their names are What and Why and When*
> *And How and Where and Who.*

For Kipling, these self-directed questions were intended to open up the subject, to draw out facts or ideas.

This is the first part of the process, and the second part is, of course, seeking answers to the questions, answers which make as much sense as possible. Most of the rest of this book goes into these processes in more detail, but for the moment it is worth emphasizing the importance of *asking the right question*. We tend to seek direct answers to self-imposed questions, so consider how Sam might have reflected on one of her training courses.

If it went entirely according to plan and expectations, then her question might have been: was it OK? This is a closed question, and in this case would obviously prompt the response – yes, in which case she could leave it there. Alternatively, she could follow it with the open question: why was this so? What actions before or during the course contributed to it going as she expected? Was she lucky: had some shortcomings she knew about (shortage of materials, uncertain grasp of some element of the course content, for example) not been exposed? Mulling over these questions, and the answers they evoke, would give Sam the material to answer the final question: what will I do next time?

If, on the other hand, there were big surprises, Sam's hopes had been dashed, and she generally regarded it as a bit of a disaster, the self-questioning could go along the lines of: why was this so? Did she have unrealistic expectations? Did the people on the course have unrealistic expectations? If so, in what way were they unrealistic? What could/should have been done to make them realistic? Were there factors entirely outside her control, for example a crisis in the organization within which she was working? If so, how could she have mitigated them? And so on, leading to Sam's final question: what will I do next time?

Looking at this sequence of questions, you can see that they often alternate between closed and open. A value judgement question produces a yes/no answer, and an open question seeks to explore why the yes or no was produced. All the answers have the potential to contribute to Sam's learning, which is encapsulated in the answer to the final question, what next?, when she applies that learning.

David Boud, a prolific researcher and writer on the subject of reflection, wrote 'What is needed is the taking up of reflection as part of work-place discourse to legitimise it and to enable work to be organised to permit it to flourish.'[3]

POINTS FOR EXPLORATION

You may not be able in the short term to have reflection legitimized in your workplace, but that in no way prevents you from starting to make opportunities for your own use. Making and taking opportunities to learn from experience is a highly personal thing, depending on the combination of you – your experience, motivation, and lifestyle, and the event(s) from which you can learn – nature, length, complexity, and so on. Here are some general questions about opportunities to consider:

- What kinds of opportunity do I already take (for example like Sam when driving home)? How can I improve on them?

---

3   David Boud (2006) in a chapter entitled 'Creating the space for reflection' (page 168). In this chapter Boud uses reflection to encompass many of the elements in the Model, not simply the reflection and insight prism.

- When I look around at colleagues, friends, and so on, what opportunities do they take which I could use as examples?

- Which, if any, of the examples given above could I adapt and adopt?

- What possibilities are there for making opportunities with other people? (The rationale for this will become more apparent in Chapter 9.)

- How can I develop an effective self-questioning technique?

CHAPTER 7

Learning Orientation

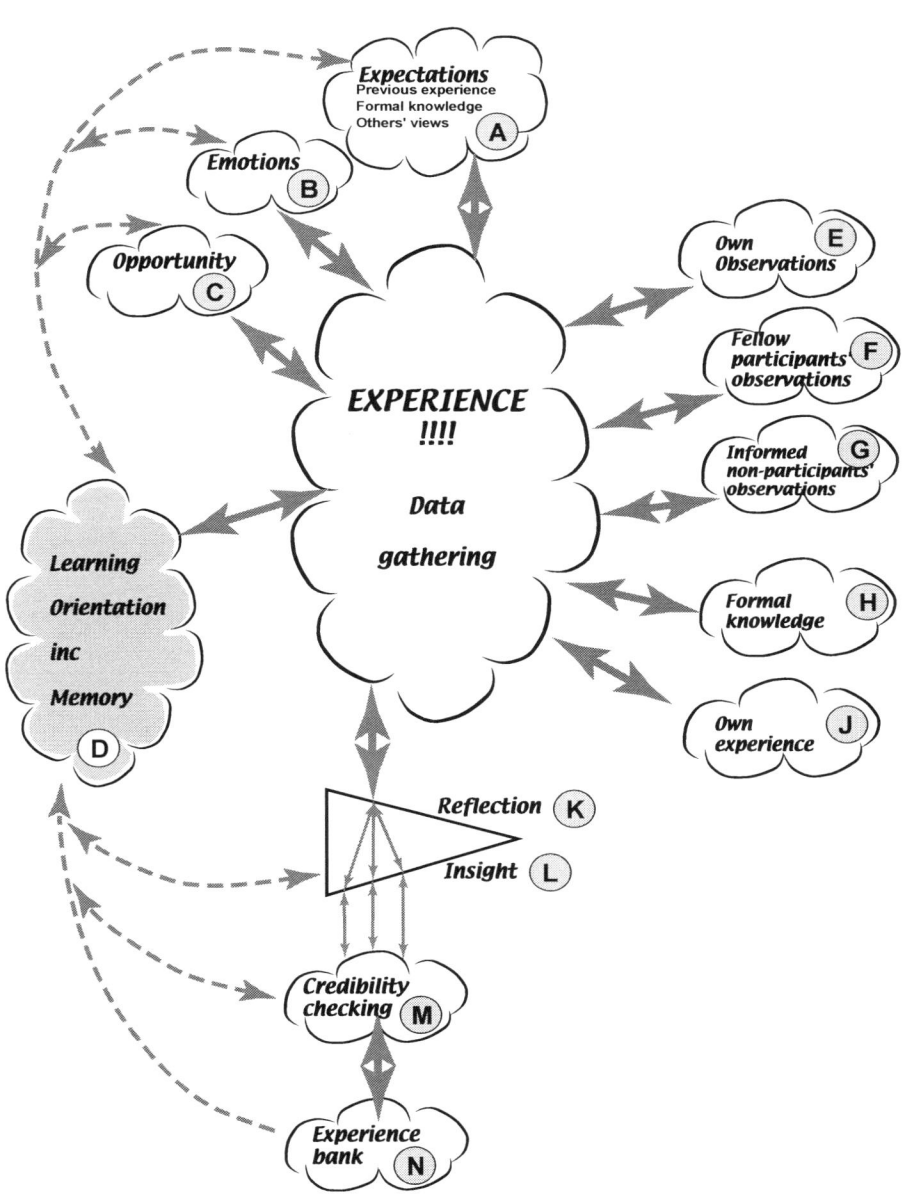

INTRODUCTION

The 31 men and women, my research colleagues, whose experiences provided the raw material for my research were a diverse bunch, with a wide age range, very varied backgrounds in terms of education, work and life experience, professional discipline, developed and under-developed economies and so on. They shared one characteristic, however, namely an interest in the ways in which people use their experiences to develop themselves, to increase their abilities in some way, or to gain more information about the world in which they were engaged.

At the start of the studies my focus was on the *events* which they were describing, seeking to understand them and discern what had been learned from them. However, very soon I was struck by different approaches my colleagues were taking, and it seemed important to recognize that people have many and varied ways of working with their experiences. Initially, I thought of these in terms of the different mindsets which they possessed, although this term did not seem fully adequate to sum up the several quite different qualities entailed in learning from experience.

Personality was another possible contributor to learning. Several colleagues had pointed to confidence and determination as being, for them, important ingredients in the learning mix. Yet this, too, was not wholly sufficient because it did not account for my earlier observations that two people with apparently similar personalities sharing a common experience could nevertheless come up with radically different learning outcomes. In a review of a building project, for example, an engineer could say she had learned about techniques and materials while an accountant could point to financial lessons. This led me to include ability as another of the inputs into learning from experience.

In addition to personality and ability, two other elements emerged as playing important roles, namely learned behaviour and memory. By 'learned behaviour' I mean ways of looking back at an event or experience, very possibly in a systematic and prescribed manner, to see what, in general terms, it offered which could be of value in the future. It is increasingly common, for example, for student courses which include practical work to contain a review period towards the end of each phase with self-directed questions such as 'what happened?', 'what went well/badly, and why?', and ' what would I do differently next time?', all of which are designed to dig into the experience and learn from it. This kind of behaviour, the routine of reviewing the experience, can be learnt and become second nature, part of our natural way of proceeding.

Memory is such an obvious part of learning from experience that it is often overlooked. Yet without our memory, both short- and long-term, whatever we learned would be of no future value. When exploring an experience we use memory to recall not only the details of the experience itself, but also a possibly huge array of other material which we may have learned from other earlier experiences, from reading in books or papers, listening to other people and so on, and then to relate the whole data, to build a comprehensive set of ideas and beliefs which are available for future use.

The key feature of all these four subelements which distinguishes them from the other elements in the 'infrastructure of reflection' is that they are relatively unchanging in the short term. While two different types of experience, encountered on the same day, say the observation of a row at work, and the pleasure of a small lottery win, evoke very different expectations, emotions and opportunities for reflection, these four subelements are unchanged during the day, probably during the week, possibly the month and perhaps for much longer. Yet they are highly significant in how we regard the two experiences.

When writing up my research I was then faced with how to encapsulate these four subelements of personality, ability, learned behaviour, and memory. Several possible terms already have particular connotations in the literature, such as learning styles, learning preferences and cognitive styles, so to avoid confusion I have used 'learning orientation' to denote that part of the infrastructure of reflection which the learner brings to his or her activities of learning from experience.

LEARNING ORIENTATION

A general description of learning orientation is that combination of a person's inborn characteristics of certain personality traits and intelligences, as developed through the various processes of socialization, together with learned behaviours, and as mediated by memory, which enable them to work with an experience in order to learn from it. The rest of this chapter is devoted to some discussion on personality, intelligences/abilities and learned behaviours, whilst Chapter 8 explores some aspects of memory, but in this section I want to point up one particular aspect of learning orientation, namely its *developing* nature.

One's learning orientation is not static or unchanging. Deep-seated personality characteristics, such as whether one is basically extrovert or introvert, probably remain stable throughout one's life, but many, many other characteristics are capable of change, growth and development and, very possibly, decay. Consider an ability in art – painting, sketching and drawing. Some people are born with great potential talent in these activities, and from an early age will seize paper and pencil or brush and produce recognizable and attractive images. From their teens onwards, they may develop this talent, professionally or as a serious hobby, or they may let it lie, and devote themselves to other things, such as academic learning, sports, or socializing. Even if they do not work with it as young men or women, they may come back to it in later life, and develop it then – although probably not in quite the same way as they would have done when much younger. Other people (I include myself), have much less talent in this kind of art, and are accordingly less likely to put much effort into developing it, yet even we, in certain circumstances, may go back to it in later life and hope to make some progress.

The essential point here is that, as individuals, we are capable of changing and developing throughout the whole of our lives as we interact with objects and other people, their ideas and what they have done or made, and that this change and development applies to our learning orientation. This, in turn, influences how, and what, we learn from experience.

To a lesser extent, perhaps, a developed ability might diminish if it is not used. Some facilities like riding a bicycle seem to stay with us for life, but others such as intricate motor skills, for example the particular manual agility needed to play a musical instrument, are often reduced if they are not used. We say we become rusty, but the good news generally is that practice usually rubs away the rust and restores our ability – generally more quickly than we took to learn it originally.

Let us look, in the rest of this chapter, in a little more detail at personality, ability, and learned behaviour.

PERSONALITY

Personality is very difficult to define, although most people have a general idea of what it means. The *Penguin Dictionary of Psychology*, for example, describes it as 'a term so resistant to definition and so broad in its usage that no coherent simple statement about it can be made'! Some people see it as so much influenced and constructed by our interactions with society, from conception onwards, that they prefer to use a word like 'identity' in its place.

A few words or phrases are useful in conveying the general idea of personality. Dictionaries typically use terms like 'distinctive or well-marked character', 'individuality', 'the sum of characteristics which distinguish a person'. For our purposes, in discussing how we learn from experience, we could think of personality as that combination of mental characteristics which influences our approach to the outside world.

Many thinkers and writers have sought to analyse personality, and have come up with a bewildering array of classifications. Some have tried to use *whole person* groupings, referring to people as, for example, 'Churchill-type', or 'Stalin-type'. Others have gone for broad subgroups of personality types; Hippocrates' cholerics is an example from the classics, and the Myers-Briggs classification into ISTJs, ENFPs, and so on is extensively used today.[1] However, much the most common analysis is by using single traits, in which a single word can describe a characteristic, such as outgoing, decisive, caring, independent. For most psychologists,[2] this single characteristic, or trait, approach is the most useful, but even then another problem arises. Do the words used to denote a trait focus on a description of it, or give an explanation of it?

Meta-studies, that is a study by a researcher into the nature and outcomes of a large number of original researches, have concluded that the trait classifications focusing on behaviour have proved the most useful. The prevailing grouping, known as the 'Big Five',[3] is given below. The headings or 'labels' for the five major trait groupings are listed together with a summary description:

1. *Neuroticism*: Assesses adjustment vs. emotional instability. Identifies individuals prone to psychological distress, unrealistic ideas, excessive cravings or urges and maladaptive coping responses.

2. *Extraversion*: Assesses quantity and intensity of interpersonal interaction; activity level; need for stimulation and capacity for joy.

3. *Openness*: Assesses proactive seeking and appreciation of experience for its own sake; toleration for, and exploration of, the unfamiliar.

---

1   *Gifts Differing* by Isabel Myers-Briggs (1995) gives a good introduction to the Myers-Briggs classification into 16 broad types, whilst *The Myers-Briggs Type Indicator* (MBTI) by Rowan Bayne reviews the ideas embodied in the MBTI and their application in education, management and therapy.
2   Hampson (1999) provides a summary of various approaches, and discusses the Big Five in some detail. Another useful introduction is that by Pervin and John (2001).
3   Two of the foremost writers in the field of personality classification are the American psychologists Costa and McCrae, whose publications alternate between this pairing and McCrae and Costa (1997).

4.   *Agreeableness*: Assesses the quality of one's interpersonal orientation along a continuum from compassion to antagonism in thoughts, feelings, and actions.

5.   *Conscientiousness*: Assesses the individual's degree of organization, persistence and motivation in goal-directed behaviour. Contrasts dependable, fastidious people with those who are lackadaisical and sloppy.

Of these five major clusters of traits, clearly openness is the one which relates most closely to learning from experience. Each of the Big Five has descriptors which characterize personalities which produce high and low scores, and for openness these are:

- High-scoring characteristics: curious, broad interests, creative, original, imaginative, un-traditional.

- Low-scoring characteristics: conventional, down to earth, narrow interests, un-artistic, un-analytical.

Thus someone with a high degree of natural curiosity, who is able to come up with new (to them) concepts or ways of doing things, and who does not feel limited to ideas or practices which are well established, is more likely to engage with a new experience, and learn from it, than someone who is less curious and more pedestrian in their thinking.

It is important to stress that these individual traits are not polarized, for example, into either curious or not curious, but rather exist in a continuum – from exceptionally curious, at one extreme, through to apathetic and passively indifferent at the other. Looking at the population as a whole, because measures of personality are based on a wide range of people of both sexes, diverse ethnic origins, all ages and so on, there is likely to be a normal distribution of, in this case, curiosity, with a very few people being extremely curious, a very few extremely incurious, and the bulk of the population distributed between these extremes. As a general rule, people with greater degrees of curiosity will tend to learn more from experience than those with lesser curiosity, for the obvious reason that they will be more inclined to have their interest aroused and to seek answers to the questions that come naturally to mind. Of course, someone might be very curious in one field and equally incurious in another; this differential application of curiosity is probably related to their abilities, which we discuss later in this chapter.

However, one's learning orientation is not based exclusively on the range of personality traits grouped together under openness. Several of the contributors to my research pointed to other personality characteristics, such as confidence, resilience and determination which they saw as helping themselves, and others, to use experience to best effect. Confidence was significant because they had to be ready to trust in the outcome of their learning, to test and use it. Someone lacking self-confidence would be less likely to rely on their conclusions. Resilience could be important in certain types of experience; Jim, who had the difficult meeting mentioned earlier, could have curled up mentally and refused to address the problem he faced, possibly blaming others around him, but he emphasized the importance in that kind of situation of bouncing back, overcoming the emotional hurt that he felt, and working out what had gone wrong and how to overcome it. Resilience is closely related to determination, another trait which, especially in dealing with profound experiences, influences learning orientation – clearly someone who is inclined to give up when faced with a problem is less likely to make progress with it than another person who can persist with their enquiries and thinking. The world of scientific discovery contains many examples of researchers who have persevered for years, even decades, before having the crucial insight which lifted them on to a new plane of thinking.

These are but three of the traits which emerged during my research; there are probably others which I did not detect, but which contribute to one's learning orientation. Within the personality classification of the Big Five, however, openness seems to cover the greatest part.

ABILITY

If personality, in its various aspects, influences our predisposition towards learning from experience, the second component of learning orientation is ability, for this tends to influence what and how much we learn. Thus, two people with similar personalities going through the same experience, for example carrying out a demanding project, might nevertheless learn very different lessons. This possibility is increasingly recognized, so that when setting up teams to study complex phenomena a consciously multidisciplinary approach is usually adopted; thus a group studying, say, crowd violence would be likely to comprise not only police but representative from the fields of psychology, social science and the magistracy, in the belief that each discipline would have some insights to contribute.

We are all born with a wide range of natural abilities, although at the time of birth they must be seen as potential abilities. The word 'ability' covers such a broad range of meanings that it is helpful to say at the outset that, in the context of someone's learning orientation, ability can be seen as the combination of intelligence and development. As such, it is a dynamic element of learning from experience, because abilities typically grow and sometimes decline throughout a lifetime. We will look in a little detail below at different types of intelligence, but to illustrate the point about growth and decline let us look at numerical intelligence. Most people are born with the capability to use numbers, but until they go to school this is not much developed. Once at school many children learn to use numbers up to the point where they can sit exams such as the GCSE, or possibly A-level. After school, numbers may become a subsidiary part of their lives, but alternatively they may become central if they pursue a career in science, engineering, accountancy, or have a strong interest in betting! Thus the way Mary, someone with a developed facility in numbers, views an experience, and seeks to learn from it, is likely to differ from Bill, someone whose numerical intelligence and development has been much less, and to this extent Mary's and Bill's learning orientations will differ. But if, for some reason, at age 30 Bill chooses to study statistics and becomes thoroughly conversant with their meanings, his learning orientation will change, and the way he approaches an experience, especially one which has a substantial numerical element, may change accordingly. Decline in numerical ability could come for both Mary and Bill with disuse over many years, and with it another shift in their learning orientations.

Intelligence is a difficult notion to pin down. One writer sums it up: 'Few concepts in psychology have received more devoted attention and few have resisted clarification so thoroughly ... Ultimately intelligence will be, conceptually, what it has always been, *the ability to profit from experience.'*[4] In western society, intelligence has come to be associated with numerical and verbal reasoning and spatial aptitude, as these three aspects have been incorporated as the basis of intelligence measurement, producing the famous (or infamous) IQ – intelligence quotient – tests used extensively for selection and development purposes.

However, many people see intelligence as much more broadly based than the three sub-parts noted above. Howard Gardner, an American educationalist, has argued[5] that there are seven intelligences, and lists them in this order:

---

4   Reber (1995) in the *Penguin Dictionary of Psychology,* pages 379–80, original emphasis.
5   See Gardner (1993).

1.   linguistic

2.   musical

3.   logical–mathematical

4.   spatial

5.   bodily–kinesthetic (for example as used in ball-sports and ballet)

6.   intrapersonal (someone's own self-awareness)

7.   interpersonal (someone's awareness of other people).

For each intelligence, Gardner discusses its core characteristics:[6] how it develops in normal individuals, including examples of people with that intelligence developed to a marked extent; how it can be affected by brain damage; and an exploration of how the intelligence can be seen in different cultures compared with his starting point of western society (European and American).

Each of these intelligences might contribute to our learning from experience, but considerations of space limit us to the briefest of summaries. Linguistic intelligence includes speaking and writing, and there are four aspects of it which have been important in human society, namely the use of language to persuade and convince; the use of words in the memory; conveying information to others – orally and in writing; and the ability of language to focus on itself, for example in giving meanings of words. The development of linguistic ability enables people to express themselves subtly, using shades of meaning which, for example, can convey information and ideas to others with great sensitivity.

It is worth observing here that, despite identifying seven definable intelligences, Gardner warns against seeing them as discrete and watertight. He says 'nature brooks no sharp discontinuities of the sort proposed here',[7] and it can readily be seen that intelligences overlap and flow into each other,

---

6   Gardner summarizes eight 'signs' of, or criteria for, an intelligence (pages 63–66). These are 'in unordered fashion': potential isolation by brain damage; the existence of idiot-savants, prodigies and other gifted individuals; an identifiable core operation or set of operations; a distinctive developmental history, along with a definable set of expert 'end-state' performances; an evolutionary history and evolutionary plausibility; support from experimental psychological tasks; support from psychometric findings; and susceptibility to encoding a symbol system.

7   Gardner (1993), page 69.

as when linguistic ability is used in conjunction with interpersonal ability, as in the last paragraph.[8]

The sign of musical intelligence is one of the first to emerge in the new-born child – exceptional musical talent may be observed as early as 3 or 4. Its principal constituents are pitch, rhythm and timbre, and while the qualities of timbre can be illustrated by most instruments its significance is paramount for most people in the human voice, which in a single note can convey a wide variety of expressions. More than any other intelligence, music can convey the emotions of the performer, so that a given tune could be played jauntily, reflectively, bombastically, or sadly. It is also very culturally related, in all three respects. Moreover, music can be associated with most other intelligences; the links with language are obvious, as with bodily–kinesthetic in dance and ballet. Logic–mathematical intelligence underpins the work of many composers, such as Bach, whilst the intra- and interpersonal intelligences find expression in solo and ensemble singing or playing.

Logic–mathematical intelligence, in contrast with music, is a slow developer in children. Gardner draws on the work of the eminent child psychologist Piaget to show how earliest experiences lead to the formation of expectations, of how objects behave in different circumstances – how a tower of wooden blocks might be stable in one construction and fall over in another. As a child realizes the permanence of objects it can then discern similarities, and thence groupings, following which quantitative understandings can develop. This enables accurate comparisons to be made, comparing and contrasting two sets of numbers, the stage reached typically by age 6 or 7, when addition, subtraction, multiplication and division can be understood. In parallel, the child appreciates causal relationships, and begins to develop the powers of classification. These processes start with external objects but gradually become internalized and abstracted. Ultimately, by adolescence, the normal child becomes capable of formal mental operations, using words, symbols, or strings of symbols, such as equations, that stand for objects. He or she is able to state hypotheses, infer their implications, and follow through consequences.

Spatial intelligence is based on the capacity to perceive the physical world accurately. Our worlds, our spaces, can range from a kitchen to an ocean, and

8   It should also be pointed out that Gardner's theory is not accepted universally. John White (1998), for example, challenges the basis of Gardner's thinking, asserting that 'the intelligences don't exist'. His arguments are set out in a pamphlet, 'Do Howard Gardner's multiple intelligences add up?' However, because in this book we are dealing with a potentially wide span of experiences it makes sense to recognize that 'intelligence' is broadly based, and not confined to things which are readily measurable.

common expressions of this intelligence can range from reproducing existing relationships, such as drawing a plan of a room, through mental modifications of existing layouts – drawing up alternative plans for the room, to conceiving entirely new rooms – as when an architect draws up the plans for an entirely new house in a unique site.

Although we use the word visualize when talking about spatial relationships, it is not necessarily a matter of actually seeing how things fit together. Gardner makes the point that blind people may possess very acute spatial intelligence, and my own work with the visually impaired confirms that they may use techniques other than sight when doing spatially exacting tasks; the sense of space when pouring a cup of tea, for example, or laying out clothes, books and other household objects, can be achieved by the senses of feeling and sound.

Spatial intelligence is used when we mentally convert a two-dimensional document such as a map of a city into the three-dimensional reality of streets, houses, parks and so on. This calls for an interpretative ability, but representative and creative spatial intelligence are used when an artist draws a country scene or a sculptor fashions a work of art. Gardner also suggests that spatial ability is used in the creation of metaphors and imagery such as Darwin's tree of life and Dalton's view of the atom as a tiny solar system. Some researchers see spatial intelligence as the pre-eminent quality needed for creative, productive thinking in any sphere, surpassing even linguistic abilities.

All the intelligences discussed so far are plainly rooted in the brain, and exercising them demands mental energy. Bodily–kinesthetic intelligence, by contrast, calls on physical energy in so far as it finds expression through the complex combination of many body parts. Supreme examples of this intelligence are to be seen in ballet, many sports performers and mime artists who use their whole bodies, but also in the limited but precise use of a few muscles, such as a surgeon wielding a scalpel. Clearly, this intelligence is often allied to other intelligences; a footballer would use spatial intelligence to get himself in the right position to shoot for goal, and a surgeon would use both spatial intelligence – how much cut, and in what direction, and logic intelligence – when planning the sequence of activities during an operation.

At a more modest level, body language entails the use of bodily–kinesthetic intelligence. An actor can convey many shades of meaning by the use of his or her shoulders, and it was said of a colleague of mine that 'he would be speechless if they cut off his hands'.

Gardner treats intra- and interpersonal intelligences together, on the grounds that they are exceptionally interrelated, while being distinct and separate. He sees the core capacity of intrapersonal intelligence as being 'access to one's own feeling of life', one's own emotions, the capacity to separate out, analyse and understand generalized – and sometimes conflicting – feelings. The ability to do this enables us to use other intelligences to inform our responses and behaviours. The failure to use this intelligence may lead someone with an incoherent mass of emotions to act blindly, possibly with adverse consequences.

While intrapersonal intelligence focuses inwardly, interpersonal intelligence looks outwards at other individuals. The core capacity here 'is the ability to notice and make distinctions among other individuals', and in particular between their moods, temperaments, motivations and intentions.[9] People who work for much of their time with other people, such as in sales or service jobs, education and medicine, need to call on this intelligence if they are to be effective: the ability to recognize behaviours and judge motivations underpins how to approach others, to meet their needs or help them develop.

Before leaving this brief summary of Howard Gardner's seven intelligences, we should note that he himself has queried whether there might actually be one or two more. In a later edition of his book[10] he questions whether there might not be three additional intelligences, namely naturalistic, spiritual and existential. Applying the eight criteria he concludes that naturalistic intelligence, which demonstrates expertise in the recognition and classification of the numerous species – the flora and fauna – of the environment, is indeed an eighth intelligence, but he is uncertain about spiritual and existential as definably separate intelligences.

Let us go back to the beginning of this section on ability, and remind ourselves that we said at the outset that ability depended on two things – intelligence, and its development. The last few pages have been dealing with intelligence, making the general point that there are quite a lot of different types of intelligence, but before finishing ability we need to discuss the part played by development.

It is a matter of common observation that intelligences are capable of growth and enlargement, but it is interesting to note that these occur in very different ways across the various intelligences. Some, such as logical–mathematical

---

9   Gardner (1993), pages 239 and 240.
10   See Chapter 4 of his revised book *Intelligence Reframed: Multiple Intelligences for the 21st Century*, Gardner (1999).

and linguistic, are helped by formal instruction, whereas others, the personal intelligences, are typically left to the individual, to her or his own methods.

A summary of the principal methods in which each intelligence can be developed is given in Figure 7.1:

Intelligence	Methods of development
Linguistic	Children learn to speak by trial and error. Formal teaching at school develops grammar and vocabulary; in adult life, awareness of other people's speech and writing enlarges vocabulary and sensitivity to shades of meaning
Musical	Awareness of rhythm and pitch starts very early in a child's life, possibly in the womb, and timbre follows shortly after. The development of certain types of musical ability, reading musical notation and playing instruments, can start around age 4 and continue into late adulthood – usually through formal teaching combined with individual practice
Logical–mathematical	As noted earlier, this intelligence develops in response to formal teaching, and does so quite slowly throughout childhood and adolescence. Judgement, the ability to know how far to apply pure logic in problematic situations probably continues to develop into the 20s[*]
Spatial	A new-born child's spatial awareness is one of its first faculties to develop as it explores the confines of its cot, and continues as it experiences other spaces and relationships. There is little formal teaching in this intelligence, although geometry and map-reading tuition are examples. The ability to make and read engineering/ architectural drawings grows with practice and experience
Bodily–kinesthetic	Like spatial intelligence, this develops naturally as a child grows to know their body. Formal teaching in, for example, ballet, sports techniques and playing musical instruments offer guidance, but mastery is the product of practice and repetition.
Intra- and interpersonal	Development in both these intelligences is almost entirely based on individual learning, through usages and reflection on their outcomes, starting immediately after birth. In recent years recognition of their importance has led to the production of some literature, for example on NLP[†]

[*] *Karen Kitchener, with colleagues, has developed a model of reflective judgement in which, in several stages, knowledge is seen at one extreme as absolute and incontrovertible, through to where, at the other extreme, knowledge is seen as contextual and open to interpretation. The capacity to develop to the latter, more mature, view takes place in most people during the late teens and 20s. See Kitchener KS and Brenner HG (1990).*

[†] *Neuro-Linguistic Programming. For an introduction to the subject, see O'Connor and Seymour (1993). Incidentally, they devote a substantial amount of space to understanding oneself, re-enforcing Gardner's point about the two intelligences being inter-dependent.*

Figure 7.1   Methods of development of intelligences

In his book on the seven intelligences, Howard Gardner makes numerous references to exemplars of exceptionally high levels of particular intelligences, such as Einstein, Mozart and TS Eliot. Superlative though these are, he says:

> *Owing to heredity, early training, or, in all probability, a constant interaction between these factors, some individuals will develop certain intelligences far more than others; <u>but every normal individual should develop each intelligence to some extent, given but a modest opportunity to do so.</u>*
>
> Gardner (1993, page 297, my emphasis).

The point to be made here, therefore, is that while one's *personality* is fairly fixed and unlikely to change much over a lifetime, *ability* – the combination of intelligence and development – is far from fixed. There are numerous examples of people in later years working on one or more intelligences which had remained largely dormant throughout their working lives, and through enlarging their capacity in some respects, being able to learn more from their overall life experiences. Of course, some abilities diminish with time, either through the ageing of the body, for example in the bodily–kinesthetic field as muscles and joints lose their strength and flexibility, or from disuse. The old adage of 'use it or lose it' probably applies to all the intelligence abilities. This apart, given appropriate personality traits, such as determination and the application of other intelligences, the diminishing effects of ageing can be largely overcome, which is good news for those approaching the 'seventh age' of mankind.

Although the general thrust of this book is about the learning that can be derived from informal experiences, that is to say experiences which have not been planned, it is worth noting that many academic courses and programmes incorporate experiential events as vehicles on which to develop desired skills, aptitudes and abilities. An exceptional, perhaps extreme, example is a course run by the US Air Force Academy whose final project includes launching a small satellite and placing it in earth's orbit![11] The required educational outcomes, expressed in terms of desired intellectual capabilities of the Academy's graduates, are to produce officers who, in addition to possessing breadth – and some depth – of knowledge in established academic disciplines:

- are intellectually curious

- can communicate effectively

11 'Implementing experiential learning: it's not rocket science' by Martin J Hornyak, Steve G Green, and Kurt A Heppard (2007).

- can frame and resolve ill-defined problems

- can work effectively with others

- are independent learners

- can apply their knowledge and skills to the unique tasks of the military profession.

This appears a neat summation of a learning orientation which is well-suited to learning informally, albeit developed in a formal academic programme.

LEARNED BEHAVIOURS

In the introductory section above on *learning orientation*, I said that:

> *'learned behaviours' meant relatively formal ways of looking back at an event or experience, very possibly in a systematic and prescribed manner, to see what, in general terms, it offered which could be of value in the future (page 60).*

These behaviours, or ways of looking back, can become so much part of our ways of working, or indeed being, that they merge in with our personalities and abilities to influence our approach to learning from experience. Thus to give a rather downbeat example, someone might have a fairly closed and incurious personality, and relatively little ability in a relevant field, and yet learn quite a lot from an experience because they had acquired some useful techniques which enabled them to draw out some lessons from an experience. It seems reasonable, therefore, to include these learned behaviours along with personality and ability as part of someone's learning orientation.

So what are these learned behaviours or useful techniques? Essentially, they are review procedures, ways of looking back on an event, seeking to note what happened and drawing out the various things that made them happen, and checking that the lessons learned were reliable. They contribute to the overall processes of reflection, and are potentially very valuable contributors to learning because they focus so closely on particular experiences.

Many organizations have formal review procedures. One of the first examples was in the Army, when after battles, skirmishes or other engagements with an enemy it became the practice to analyse what had happened, what worked well and how to consolidate those activities, and what went badly – and how to avoid them. Towards the end of the First World War, after the Allied armies had suffered calamitous setbacks from 1914 to 1917, officers of all ranks were reviewing the various aspects of their strategy and tactics and introducing changes which, during the Hundred Days between August and November 1918, led to victory.[12] The same approach is adopted by many industrial and commercial companies in post-project reviews when, after major construction projects or other innovations, a formal examination is made of all aspects so that performance in subsequent projects can be improved.

The point of mentioning these reviews in the context of individual learning is that after someone has been involved in several such processes over a few years, the procedures of review are likely to become embedded in that person's learning orientation. So regardless of their personality and ability, the carrying out of reviews becomes a natural behaviour, and can be used extensively for future learning.

It is this principle that lies behind the incorporation of learning logs, learning diaries, reflective assignments and the like which have been introduced as an important part of student courses. The belief, born of experience, is that the use of this type of review is doubly beneficial. Thus the student, whether they are studying engineering, PR, or nursing, who undertakes some sort of reflection or review after a project is likely to learn not only how that project could be carried out better in the future, but also something of how they actually learned the lessons contained in the project. A good example of this in my own experience was Veronica, whose job was that of managing a busy GP surgery practice, and who was studying for a certificate in management: she kept learning logs of four projects in her practice, as result of which her repertoire of techniques for innovation increased, but she also understood herself better and was able to build on her newly learned strengths. As a matter of interest, she chose to structure her logs in the four phases of Kolb's learning cycle described in Chapter 2, namely experience – describing what happened; reflection – pondering on how and why things happened; generalizing – drawing some conclusions from it; and action – planning her next moves and testing/experimenting with these conclusions in the future.

---

12 An interesting account of various changes made as a result of these reviews is given by Andrew Syk (2004). He shows how the creeping artillery barrage, the new machine-gun barrage, limited and attainable objectives, better integration between the army and air-force, a more decentralized command structure, and improved communications all contributed to the final victory.

In the last chapter we met Kipling's little verse in which he attributes his learning to the ability to ask himself questions. It bears repetition:

I keep six honest serving-men
(They taught me all I knew);
Their names are What and Why and When
And How and Where and Who.

Thus, for Kipling and for us, looking back at the project, experience, or event: what happened? Why did it happen? and, possibly, why did something else not happen? When, at what time and in what sequence, did it happen? Where did it happen, and who was involved? What lessons does if offer? And how could/should I use them in the future? These review questions are intended to dig into the experience and bring out into the open some of its influences and dynamics.

These questions can be kept in one's head, but they could also be written down in notes, logs, diaries, mind maps, or whatever form of writing suits one best. The advantages of writing are twofold. First, the very act of writing is, for most people, an aid to precision and to being comprehensive. Second, having written it, it can then be used in the future to remind you of what you thought of the experience at the time – or at least at the time you wrote the note. Both these merits are worth the trouble of writing, although it has to be admitted that for many people the act of writing is more tedious than it's worth. The trick is to find a way of minimizing the tedium while still capturing and retaining the essentials of the experience.

One final thought on writing self-notes or logs. While it is a good idea to get down on paper one's thoughts on an experience as soon as possible after the event, it is also generally even more helpful to return to the paper in a day or so. This is because one's mind continues to review things subconsciously, and if you return to your first thoughts you will probably find that there are one or two important extra points you want to make. (We will look at this phenomenon more closely in Chapter 11.)

If inertia, the dislike of the tedium, is one barrier to reviewing, it is not alone. For many people there are some very real 'lacks': they lack the time, the skill, the support from others, the opportunity to step aside from the pressure of events. There are also some assumptions or presuppositions which get in the way, such as that people like me don't do this sort of thing, that it isn't worth the effort, that learning is not really like this, or that having tried it once and found it of no value it should not be considered again.

These counter factors are too many and too personal to be dealt with individually, and the weight you put on them will probably be influenced by your personality. The most apposite comment is probably to adapt the saying well-known in education circles: 'If you think learning is too difficult, try ignorance!'. The review process is so well established that we discount it at our peril.

Finally, for many people, a learned behaviour that is immensely helpful in making sense of experience is that of chatting about it with one or two other people. This is so significant in experiential learning that it is a major topic in a later chapter, but it is worth mentioning it here. Making time for a quick review at the end of a meeting or other event with someone whose judgement and perceptiveness are valued is a practice which provides other perspectives which may complement or challenge your own. It will also help in fixing it in your memory – the subject of the next chapter.

POINTS FOR EXPLORATION

Personality: It is quite difficult to be objective about our own personalities, particularly if our intrapersonal skills are on the low side. This being so, it is usually very helpful to take some of the self-report psychometric questionnaires, such as Myers-Briggs, which are intended to reveal, as objectively as possible, some of our basic attitudes and preferences. My experience of such 'instruments' is that, when they receive feedback on them, respondents usually find them to be highly perceptive, using phrases like 'uncannily accurate'.

Another way of exploring the personality aspects of learning from experience is to look outwards, at other people who seem to be very good, or very bad, at such learning.

- What is it about them that makes them so good/bad?

- How does openness/closed-ness show?

- Are they naturally curious? How does that curiosity show itself?

- To what extent are they determined, resilient, and focused?

- What other traits do they show which appear to help them?

- What was getting in the way, inhibiting them from learning?

- What could break down these barriers?

A variant on this theme is to do it with a trusted partner, in which you describe your partner's learning behaviours and they describe yours. It helps if you can be very different, because you will then reveal to each other areas where there is scope for growth and change. At the very least it will increase self-awareness. It does not need to be a one-off event; if you are working together, on a project, for example, feedback can be based on an actual event and very quick, so that over time self-awareness can grow significantly. Moreover, you will often think of a facet of feedback a few hours, even day or two, later, and offer it next time you meet.

Ability: Most people have a greater awareness of their abilities than of their personality, but the same technique of observing others, and possibly working with a partners, holds good. An important, and sometimes crucial, point to remember is that for much work, many projects, several of Gardner's intelligences are involved. The trick is to see how many, and in what ways!

So, in reviewing an experience, the self-directed questions could be:

- Which intelligences/abilities did it require?

- How able was I in them?

- What could I do to improve in abilities that threatened to let me down?

Again, working with a partner can be very helpful, as they identify strengths you did not know you possess, and limitations which would repay effort.

Learned behaviours: Working in the ways suggested above would be examples of learned behaviours! You would be reviewing not only an actual experience, but your, and possibly your partner's, way of dealing with that experience. As such it would be *very* reflective practice.

Again, observing others, to see how they review their experiences, can offer useful suggestions of techniques which could work for you.

CHAPTER 8

Memory

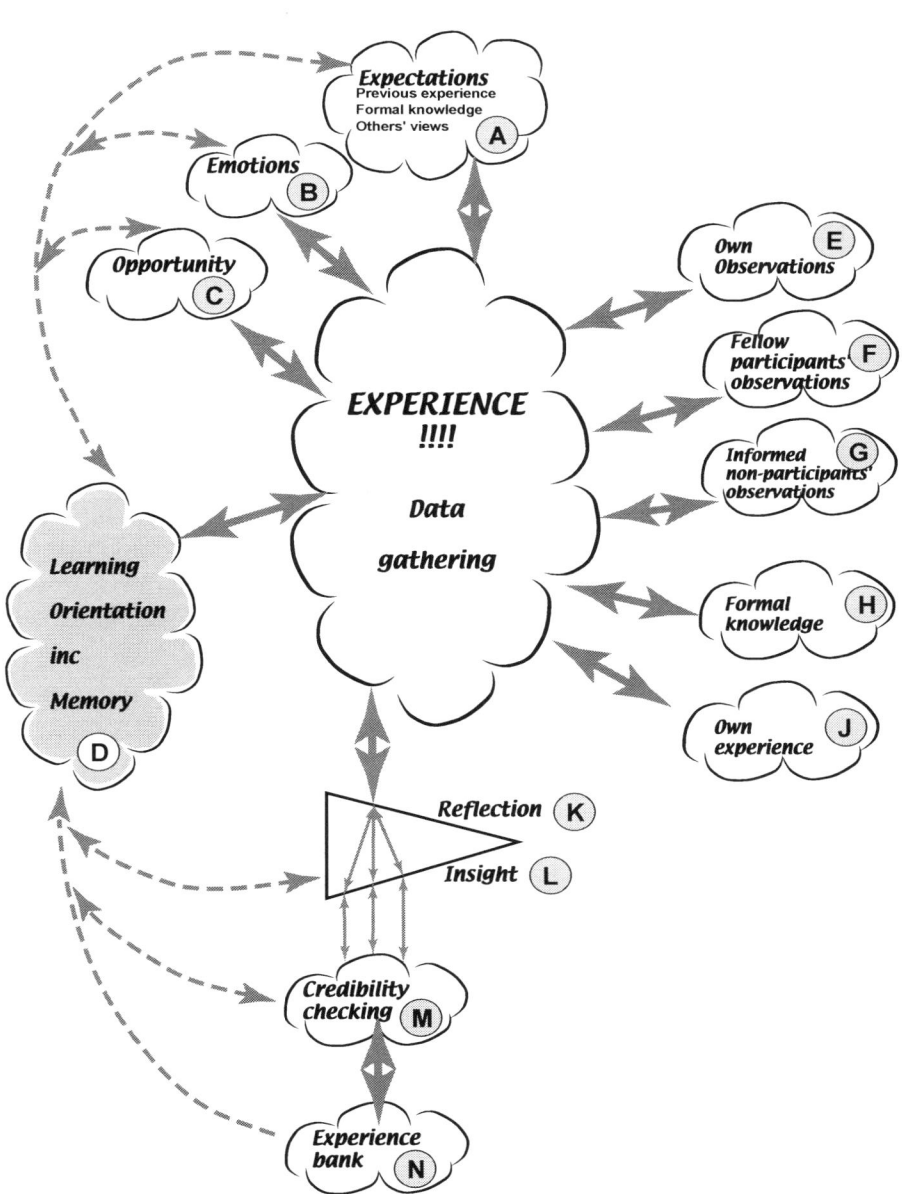

INTRODUCTION

The place – and importance – of *memory* in making sense of, and learning from, experience is often overlooked or taken for granted. Yet without it any learning would be, literally, useless.

The truth of this was illustrated by the extremely sad case of Clive Wearing, a classical musician by profession, who had suffered a viral illness which had attacked his brain and left him with no short-term memory. Living in a very sheltered environment, when his wife visited him he would be delighted to see her, but if she left him for a few moments he would be equally delighted to see her on her return, because he had no recollection of her earlier arrival. She said of him that his world 'now consists of a moment, with no past to anchor it and no future to look ahead to'.[1]

Someone with a normal memory who travels to a new city by train might use a street map to find their hotel, but having done so once would probably not need to use the map again to make the same journey. Unless long and complex, the configuration of streets, buildings, and traffic flows would probably remain in memory for at least a few days, and could be used to retrace the same journey, and probably as the starting point for the location of, say, a shop which lay slightly off the known, and remembered, route. We take this kind of experience for granted.

Equally most people acknowledge that their memories are fallible, at least to some extent, so when considering learning from experience the question naturally arises: to what extent can we rely on our memory as a basis for our learning? This leads to other questions: how does memory work? And what can we do to improve it? These are big questions, and can only be touched on in this chapter, but enough can be said to reassure ourselves and provide some help.[2]

CAN WE RELY ON OUR MEMORIES?

Experiments have shown that memories of events can change over time, and also that they can be influenced by third parties suggesting false information. Thus if we are shown a film of a minor road accident, as time passes our recollection of peripheral detail, such as the colour of a car, becomes hazy and

---

1   The case of the musician, Clive Wearing, is described by Blakemore (1988) page 55. Deborah Wearing, his wife, has written a moving account of his, and her, experiences in *Forever Today* (2005).

2   For a fuller account see Alan Baddeley's book *Essentials of Human Memory (1999)*.

open to error. If someone suggests false information, perhaps the presence (or not) of other unaffected vehicles, we are liable to accept such falsehoods and build them into our mental picture.[3]

However, these were *peripheral* details rather than the central features of the event, which remained unchanged and accurate. More importantly, in real life we are dealing not with experiments but with our own experience which, as noted in Chapter 5, usually is associated with some sort of emotion – and it is the strength of the emotion which helps to keep the memory in our minds. In the two illustrations given in Chapters 1 and 2, Jeannie and Jim remembered the incidents from which they learned; Jeannie may well not recall who else was present when she met the bereaved mother, and Jim probably would not remember what the people in his difficult meeting were wearing, but the central issues of how, for Jeannie, to deal with bereaved people, and, for Jim, to prepare for potentially difficult arguments, stayed with them clearly and vividly for years afterwards.

It would be wrong to imply that memories of core events are infallible, because we can all make mistakes, transferring people, places, events, forgetting completely some, even central, experiences and drawing wrong conclusions. However, assuming we have normal brains, that is we do not suffer from the kind of tragic illness mentioned in the introduction or from Alzheimer's disease, it seems realistic to assume that our capacity for memory serves us sufficiently well to enable us to have confidence in our ability to learn from experience.

HOW DOES MEMORY WORK?

The human brain is an amazingly complex organ, and neuroscientists have discovered that it has at least 35 different locations where memories are processed or stored. Not surprisingly, therefore, the simple question: 'How does memory work?', cannot receive a correspondingly simple answer. Consider three different types of memory: how to ride a bicycle, how to find your way in a city, and how to solve quadratic equations (assuming you learnt them at school). The actions required to do each of these draw on different parts of the brain, which accounts for the fact that physical damage to a part of the brain can lead to the loss of some functions but not others. The musician mentioned above who completely lost his short-term memory, for example, could nevertheless remember works he had learned before his illness, and conduct his choir in them very capably.

---

3   Elizabeth Loftus' experiments are described in Baddeley, pages 205–206.

Psychologists have offered several theories explaining how memory works, most of which are based on the observation that we tend to remember clusters of related things. One of the best known is the *schema* theory.[4] 'Schema' is the Greek word for 'form', 'shape' or 'plan', and it builds on the idea that individual memories are collected and organized in such a way that, not only can they be used together to inform action or further thought, but new information can be added and incorporated.

Examples of schemas (the correct plural of the Greek schema is 'schemata', but popular usage is 'schemas'), which many people have developed from their own experience relate to: airports, restaurants, committee meetings, one's own home, petrol stations and children's parties. Let us look in a little detail at airports, as seen from the point of view of an ordinary passenger. As experienced travellers, when we use an airport we bring together a large number of individual memories, such as how and where to buy a ticket (through an agent, online, and so on), how early to arrive (early for an international flight, quite late for a shuttle, but also how to adjust these ideas when, for example, terrorism checks extend arrival time), how to organize luggage (major items in suitcase for the hold, a few small items for the cabin), what to do while waiting for the flight (buy a paper, drink a coffee), and so on. Each of these relatively large elements is composed of subelements – buying a ticket would require the recollection of different payment methods, such as cheque, credit, and the important check that you can actually afford it.

Obviously, many subelements have multiple uses, such as the different payment methods when we pay for clothes, services, or other forms of transport. In the airport schema the memory of 'how to pay' is invoked when buying the ticket, and when buying a paper or coffee. Moreover, the building up of an airport schema is most probably something that is done by experience, rather than by reading a book or being given instruction; for young people it is often something that is unconsciously learned when accompanying their parents, just as earlier generations learned how to use train stations or bus stations. (There is an amusing story about the very early days of railway travel, when farmers tried to negotiate a lower fare when paying for a ticket. In the farmers' schema of payment, negotiating a price was a normal process.)

A schema is therefore a vehicle of memory, allowing an individual to organize their similar experiences for the purposes of identifying, elaborating,

---

4   Schema theory is described in Baddeley's book, but the best account I have read is in Marshall (1995). She gives an historical introduction in Chapter 1, and in Chapter 2 provides a comprehensive summary.

planning and executing the knowledge needed for a particular task. Thus in the airport schema, we might say to ourselves: we need to fly leaving from airport X, that is *identification*. We draw together information relevant to X, how to get there, any special procedures, and so on – *elaboration*. We say: how long will it take to travel there, how early should we arrive, how much money will we need actually at the airport and so on – *planning*. And then we act on the drawing together of all our memories of airports – *execution*.

It is worth noting that although the examples of schemas given above are mostly based on experiential learning rather than on didactic learning, that is what we acquire from books, lectures, articles or direct instruction (sources which I have called *Formal Knowledge* in the Model), schemas may consist entirely of memories derived exclusively from didactic learning. Thus a student learning history may initially build up a schema, or series of schemas, on, say, the English Civil War, which are composed entirely from information from books and lessons, although later they might add to this schema information gained first hand from visiting battlefields or examining contemporary accounts. Very often, a schema may be formed at the outset from didactic material, such as a cook working from recipes or an engineer from tables of strengths of materials and structures, but in time and with experience those schemas may develop and be substantially enhanced by experience of preparing meals or building bridges.

This discussion on schemas goes some way to answering the question of how memory works. We organize small, and sometimes large, items of information into relationships where they are usable, or possibly just sufficiently different and interesting as to be memorable for their own sakes – for example, trivia for pub quizzes – and because we are fallible, sometimes we fail to use the schema, for example when, although I know that parking my car requires certain coins, I forget to take them.

IMPROVING MEMORY

It seems to be a characteristic of the human condition that people lament their poor memories. Actually, it is really adults, rather than people in general, because children are rarely concerned with their capacity to remember. Where did I leave my book? What is that person's name? Why did I come upstairs? These are all questions based on the failure to recall things which are stored in our long-term or short-term memories. Compared with the wealth of information which we *can* recall, it seems over-critical to chastise ourselves for minor lapses.

However, the inability to remember facts or ideas can, at a more serious level, be disastrous. Anyone, child or adult, tackling an exam and being unable to remember the salient information which underlies the answer to questions is bound to fail, and exams are an extreme example of the tests which we face throughout life. Anyone with a responsible job will be required, from time to time, to draw on their memory to solve an immediate problem. So helping the memory to function efficiently is clearly a worthwhile endeavour.

At the risk of stating the obvious, in order to remember something one has to learn it in the first place, so let us look at ways of learning. In this context, learning does not necessarily mean *understanding*, although it is obviously preferable. As a child I learned my 'times table' by rote, but it was only as an adult I understood that, say,

> $7 \times 9 = 63$ *was really saying that seven added to itself nine times came to 63. In the meantime, and since, because I knew the 'seven times table' off by heart I could respond without hesitation to the need to multiply numbers by, for example, seven.*

The trick for most people in embedding data in their brains is to build up a schema in which the information being learned is organized in some manner. Thus if we are learning French, the 'verbs schema' will almost certainly start by establishing the shape of regular verbs such as *donner*, *dormir*, and *vendre*, presenting them in the present, imperfect, future and other common tenses; when we know and can recall these, other regular verbs can be processed easily. Alongside these, we will learn *être* and *avoir*, and all the other verbs of increasing degrees of irregularity. Some verbs which are compounds of others can be readily understood, but others appear to have no logical structure and just have to be learned. Gradually the schema will be built up to include all verbs in common usage.

Sometimes there is no logical basis for forming a schema and we have to invent one. A common way of doing this is to devise a mnemonic, that is a device such as a catchy phrase or verse designed solely to act as a memory jogger. Perhaps the best known is 'Richard of York gave battle in vain' to remember the colours of the rainbow – red, orange, yellow, green, blue, indigo, violet. Although it is many years since I was learning A-level biology, the mnemonic for remembering the cranial nerves sticks in my mind:

> *On old Olympus topmost top*
> *A fat eared gremlin gives a hop.*

Thus the nerves are, in the order they arise from the brain of a mammal – olfactory, optic, oculomotor, trochlear, trigeminal, abducent, facial, stato-acoustic, glossopharyngeal, vagus, accessory, hypoglossal; the initial letters of the words in the couplet correspond to the initial letters of the nerves (except for stato-acoustic, where ear and acoustic correspond, and 'gives' and 'vagus' correspond). The value of the couplet is, therefore, that once one knows the nerve names it gives a clue as to the first letter of (almost) each nerve, reminds one that there are 12 nerves, and presents them in the order in which they enter the brain. Medical students, for example, who have to learn a great deal of factual material, which is often entirely arbitrary such as Latin names for body parts, frequently rely on mnemonics of this kind to help them recall stuff they have learned. The more pithy, or even vulgar, the better!

But this is not the end of the problem. Even when some new mass of data is sorted out satisfactorily and built into a schema, it will almost certainly begin to disappear from one's memory. Even though I learn my couplet, and using it can come up with 'olfactory, optic, oculomotor' and so on, within minutes of having it fixed in my mind I will start to forget it – although the mnemonic (if I can remember it) will act to some degree to retard the loss. Experiments have shown that retention times for new material, especially when it is very different from anything we knew hitherto, is extremely short; some will be forgotten within minutes, and most within hours or a day or two.[5]

The good news, however, is that there are ways of avoiding this loss. In a word, they depend on *revision*.[6] Consider the following anecdote:

Using as Remembering

Some years ago I was visiting a senior colleague, Derek, when he asked for help. We had been together a month earlier negotiating an agreement with a trade union, but he was now lamenting the fact that he could remember almost nothing of its contents. By contrast, he could remember an agreement he had negotiated several years earlier, almost to the last detail.

---

5   Baddeley's book reports some of the classic experiments in the this field, in Chapter 6 on Forgetting.
6   A helpful book on using your memory is Tony Buzan's *Using Your Memory* (2003), one of a suite of books based on his original *Use Your Head* book which accompanied his memorable TV series in 1974.

I had recently seen Tony Buzan's programme on memory on TV and was able to help him, both on the specifics of the recent agreement, and to reassure him that he was not becoming senile. In the recent agreement, Derek's responsibility had ended when it had been concluded, and in the following weeks he had been engaged on entirely different issues, whereas I had continued to work with it. He had had no occasion even to think of it. Following the earlier agreement, however, he had had to implement it, explain it, interpret it defend it, and later to add to it over the ensuing months.

The key was the difference in Derek's use of the two agreements, which amounted to 'revision' in its literal sense, that is of seeing or using again. The recent one had not been used at all, so even though it was only a month old, all its content had eroded from his memory. The earlier one, by contrast, had been used many times in various ways, and each time he had used it he had 'topped up' his memory of its contents. Derek would probably remember much of it all his life.

Tony Buzan showed how revision works using the graph in Figure 8.1.

Experiments have shown that once we have learned something we would normally retain the whole of it for only a short time – measured in minutes or, at the most, hours. After that, as time passes we are likely to be able to recall less and less, until after a few days we would remember only a small percentage of the original 100 per cent. If we check our memory after, say, two hours, find that we have already forgotten perhaps 10 per cent, and make a point of revising, that is re-learning that 10 per cent, *the rate at which we forget reduces*, that is we remember more. The really good news is that we don't need to revise every two hours; revision at decreasing intervals is all that is needed. So in the graph in Figure 8.1, having revised after a few hours, the second revision is after two or three days, the third after one week, another after a month, and so on. Each time we need to top up our memory by a relatively small amount, so that in the longer term, many months or years later, our recollection of the totality, the 100 per cent, of what we originally learned, will be high.

Derek, in the example 'Using as Remembering' had 'revised' his memory of the earlier agreement every time he had used it, so that years later he could recall almost all of it. Taking as an example the cranial nerves mentioned above, if I learn them to the point where I can readily write down each nerve in the order in which they arise from the brain, in order to 'fix' them in my memory I would revise them – that is, write them down from memory – after a few

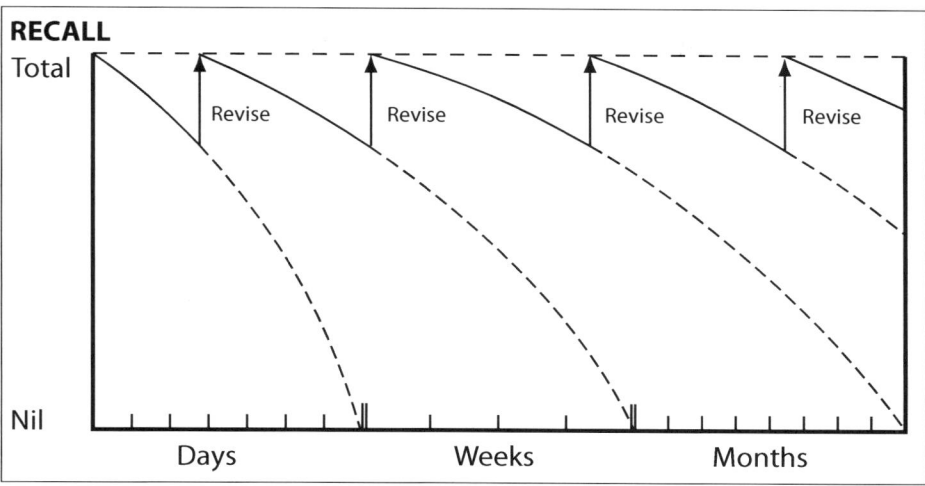

RECALL

Total

Revise   Revise   Revise   Revise

Nil

Days   Weeks   Months

Figure 8.1   Rates of loss of learned material

hours, reminding myself of the one, or perhaps two, I had forgotten; repeat the process the next day, then after a couple of days, then the next week, next month, and three months later, after which I would probably remember them for a long time. And of course, the mnemonic, the jokey couplet, would be an immense help in jogging my memory for both the first letter of (almost) each nerve and the order in which they arise.

I wish I had known this information about revision when I was a student! It doesn't relieve one of the task of learning in the first place, but it does mean that something which is learned, perhaps, six months before an exam can be kept almost complete in one's memory, available for use when answering questions. I have used it for the occasional exam taken as an adult in recent years, and it works.

In normal life, of course, we do not face the artificiality of exams, but 'revision' works equally well. We tend to remember the phone numbers we use regularly, the names of colleagues, as cooks, the recipes and amounts of dishes we prepare regularly, and so on. The equivalent of a mnemonic could be a bad experience; the memory of a tasteless dish may remind us not to forget the salt in a recipe.

This last example brings us back to schemas in the context of memory. If we are accustomed to cooking we will have a general, overarching schema for cooking embracing preparing, boiling, roasting, baking and so on. Within this general schema there will be specific schemas for preparing and boiling vegetables, roasting meat (unless we are vegetarian), baking bread or cakes, and within each of these our memory will inform our actions for each of the stages needed. Thus we would probably rely entirely on memory for cooking most vegetables, but when it comes to baking a particular type of sponge, say for a Swiss roll, our memory may well tell us that significant details such as quantities and procedures are too important to be left to memory, and we would consult the recipe books. However, if we bake Swiss rolls frequently the 'revision' implicit in repetition would enable us to rely on memory at each step.

CONCLUSION

This chapter on memory is the last chapter on the infrastructure of learning, the various elements that exist within each one of us which influence how we learn from experience. We said earlier that 'infrastructure' means 'inner structure, or structure of component parts', and I hope it can be seen that an individual's memory is an important part of what and how he or she learns from an experience.

We rely on our schemas to make sense of what is going on around us and to be part of it. An experienced cook, tasting a familiar dish prepared by someone else, might identify a new ingredient, say a herb or spice, and think that it improved the dish and could be copied. The cook's well-developed schema for cooking in general and that dish in particular enabled her or him to discriminate finely and learn from the experience.

To give a contra-example, I wonder what I would learn if I were caught up in the sort of gun battle we see on TV screens when an invading army is capturing a town, house by house. I have absolutely no schema for close-quarters fighting of this kind, and would probably be terrified and paralysed, and would learn nothing – beyond that I hated it. By contrast, an experienced soldier, that is someone with a well-developed schema for such fighting, who is involved in the same incident could easily learn from it; despite the noise, the sights and smells of devastation, he might notice some detail which influenced all his future conduct in such fighting. Training is the most valuable method of building up schemas, so that even before a soldier goes into battle for the first time he should have been exposed to all the sensations it entails, be familiar with them, and able to distinguish between phenomena, such as, perhaps, the differences between different kinds of rifle fire.

POINTS FOR EXPLORATION

- It would be interesting to think of one or two schemas for normal activities, such as filling a car with petrol, and see where there are overlaps with other schemas, such as paying for other products/ services

- Test the 'memory graph' (Figure 8.1) by learning something new, just for the sake of it, and checking how revision helps to keep it alive in memory. (Suggestions: the Chinese dynasties; the line-up of a football team of the past; the names and titles of *all* the current members of the Cabinet; the titles of the top pop songs of four years ago.)

CHAPTER 9

Observations of Experience

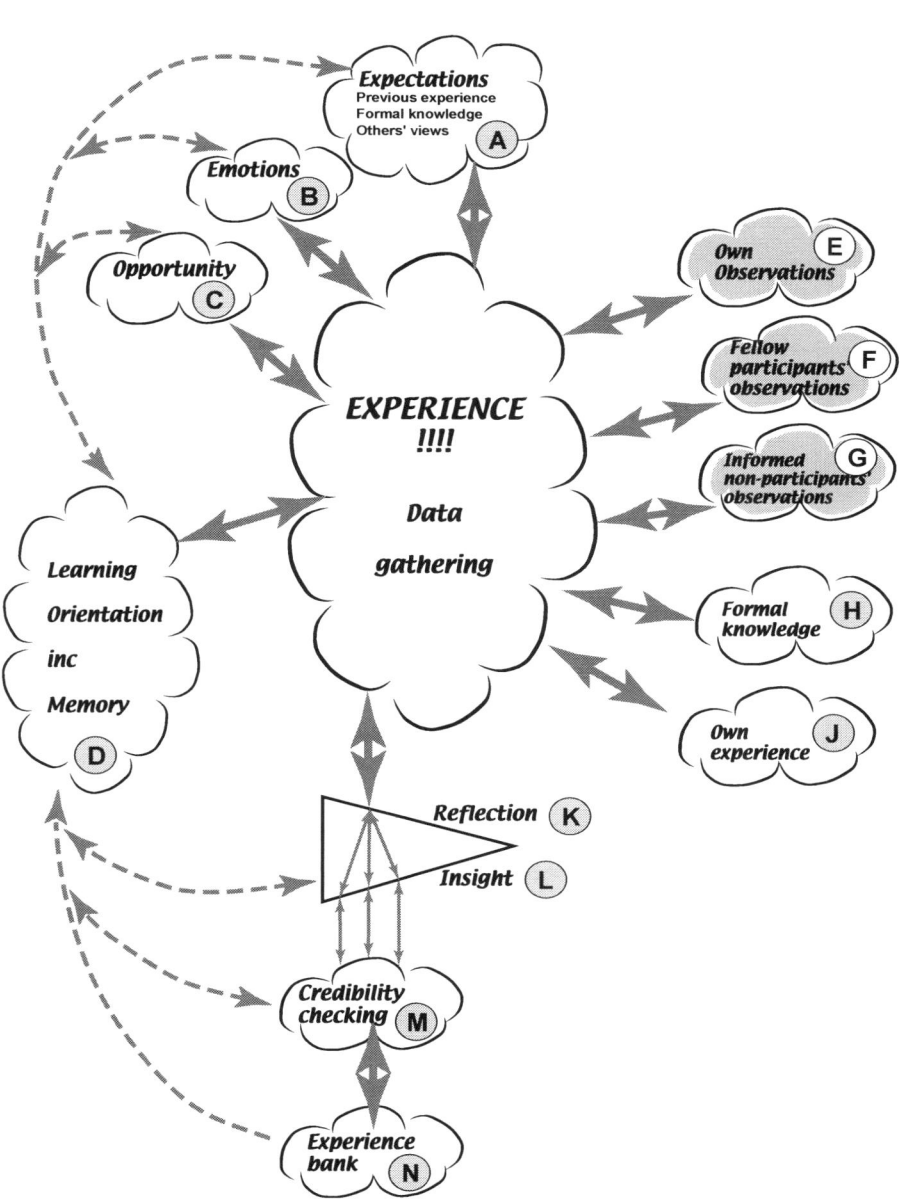

INTRODUCTION

Finally, we arrive at the experience itself. It may seem strange at first sight that in a book on learning from experience, the experience should be addressed more than halfway through, but I hope that the preceding five chapters have pointed to the crucial and individual contribution each element makes to our sense-making process. Moreover, because we ourselves change with time, the sense we make of, and the lessons we learn from, an experience at one age might be quite different from those we derive from a very similar experience years later.

When we consider an experience, such as Jeannie meeting her bereaved friend (in Chapter 1) or Jim pondering his distressing meeting (Chapter 2), we naturally go back over the event, identifying key moments in our mind's eye, phrases we heard or said, the body language of the principal actors (that is, those who were part of the action), and anything that strikes any of our five senses. The participants I interviewed in my research often gave compelling narratives of what had happened to them or in their presence, re-living incidents which might have occurred many years earlier. However, as we discussed their accounts, which they naturally presented in first-person terms – they were, of course, *their* experiences – it often emerged that when they were making sense of the events they brought in other people.

Often, these other people were part of the same experience. In the very first interview, Rick, who was working at the time in a City finance firm, described how he had been eased out of his job, despite exemplary performance, by an outsider who was taking over the firm. As his account progressed it became clear that he was not alone in his predicament; others were also feeling the threat of dismissal, and it became clear that Rick was part of a small group of *fellow-participants* who would meet up after work in the pub and discuss their situation. The sense that Rick made of the experience, the lessons he learned that influenced his subsequent career, were undoubtedly personal to him – but they embraced observations, thoughts, ideas and beliefs that had been put forward by others in that pub group.

While Rick was able to learn from his experience with inputs from other participants in the same experience, Anne, another early interviewee, pointed to another source of guidance, the *informed non-participant*. For Anne, this person was someone who had had the same type of experience that she was going through and was able, by a combination of questioning and commenting, to illuminate some of her problems.

So as I listened to the accounts which my research colleagues told me, I found that in the majority of cases the lessons they had learned had been far from solo efforts. Inputs had come from fellow participants and from informed non-participants, in addition to their own personal observations and thoughts. These are all live, active and interactive sources, so this chapter deals with some of the ways that they can be used to make the most sense, to derive the greatest learning from an experience.

Each of the three elements E, F, and G in the Model is discussed below, to show how they can add to the data on which we can work. Finally, however, the point will be made that they are often far from discrete and separate. On the contrary, one can link in to another, re-enforce or challenge another. Learning from an experience is rarely a sudden, simple activity – unless the experience is correspondingly sudden and simple – and as time passes our own observations may be stimulated and increased as a result of an input from, say, a fellow participant's observations. So the final section touches on the possibilities of 'linked observations'.

OUR OWN OBSERVATIONS

There can be no doubt that we learn most from our own experiences, the things we did, that happened to us, that we saw, heard, felt and so on. From the moment we are born we start to relate to our environment, watching, hearing, touching, smelling and tasting it, so that we gradually build up a picture of what our world is like and how we need to live in it.

Although school, and possibly further or higher education, puts the emphasis on learning from books, teachers, and other external sources, in our parallel lives outside education, in leisure activities, with friends, on holidays and in our homes, experience continues to offer important lessons. When we enter the world of work, learning from experience comes back into the foreground; few jobs are carried out exclusively by reference to a manual. As the boss of a friend of mine said when my friend arrived at his first job after a university degree in engineering: 'Good, now you can really start to learn!' My friend wondered what he meant, but over the next months and years he realized – the theoretical knowledge acquired at university needed to be allied to a wide variety of other, practical knowledge needed to turn concepts into reality. All this latter knowledge was founded in doing things, usually succeeding but sometimes making mistakes, and deriving the lessons this practice offered.

How is this done? We have already seen a large part of the answer in the chapter on *opportunity*, when I mentioned Kipling's 'six honest serving men' – the questions: what? why? when? how? where? who? – to which we could add the seventh: which? These are open questions, that is they invite multiple answers. So the question 'what happened?' could easily elicit several, perhaps many, responses. '*What* happened in that meeting (that was so awful, so unproductive)? could prompt answers such as 'people rambled', 'the chair dominated it', 'there were no clear conclusions', 'X lost his temper' and so on.

Similarly, the '*why*?' question could lead to several responses: 'people were unprepared', 'the chair likes to hear her own voice', 'no one tried to sum up', and 'X felt we were addressing the wrong problem'. Although what? and why? are often the most natural questions to ask oneself, is worthwhile thinking of each of Kipling's questions because they can lead to new and productive trains of thought. '*When* did X lose his temper?' could lead to realization that it was only after he had tried to pose the problem as he saw it. '*How* did the chair deal with X?' could offer some tips on how, or how not, to handle that kind of incident. '*Where* was the meeting held, and *who* was sitting next to whom?', '*who* was there, and *who* should have been there?', and *which* agenda items were the most difficult (or easy)? – all could have some implications for arranging future meetings.

In this meeting example your observations are most likely to be based on the senses of sight and hearing. Other types of experience call for different senses. When chefs are being trained, they are required to smell and taste the food they are preparing at frequent intervals, so that by asking themselves questions such as 'how is it tasting?', 'what should I do to correct or enhance it?', and 'when will it go to the next stage?' they can develop the quality standards needed to be good at their job. Similarly, woodworkers learn to judge the sharpness of their tools by stroking their thumbs across the cutting edge, and gradually they build up an impression of how effectively a chisel, for example, will cut.

Asking ourselves these questions is intended to collect data from which to make sense of an experience and learn from it. It may sometimes be productive to ask a question along the lines of 'what did *not* happen?' In Conan Doyle's *The Hound of the Baskervilles*, the detective Sherlock Holmes famously asked himself why a guard dog had *not* barked: it led him to the conclusion that a murder had been committed by someone the dog knew, which in turn led to the solution of the mystery.

Obviously, when asking the 'what did *not* happen?' question, it is sensible to stay within the bounds of realism. There was no earthquake, and nobody died, and there is no point in asking why not – but these were not within the bounds of realism. The 'what/why not...?' question is worth asking when you had a strong and realistic expectation that something would happen, but it did not. So if, in the meeting above, X could usually be expected to help the chair by summing up as she saw it, but at this meeting made no such attempts, a potentially productive question would be 'Why did X not bother to sum up?' By observing her, you might conclude that she was not very well, or that she was very fed up. You could ask her afterwards, if it seemed important.

In the above examples the presumption is that the person is directly involved in the experience in some way. In the meeting example, we assume that you were part of it, contributing as appropriate, whilst the chefs were themselves learning about taste and smell, as were the woodworkers of the touch of sharp

---

Handling an Explosive Situation

Many years ago I was attending an important negotiating meeting between my company and the main union. The speaker for the company was Harry, an urbane, clever and courteous man, and the union side was led by a very experienced general secretary, Dick.

To my surprise and horror, Harry started the meeting by being rude and abusive to the other side, accusing them of discourtesy and dishonesty, using language that was completely out of character with his normal calm, considerate manner. He was not using the arguments I had expected, but was following a completely different and dangerous line.

To my equal surprise and relief, Dick reacted with equanimity. He could very reasonably have taken offence and led a walk-out of his side, but in fact he responded by addressing Harry and saying that he clearly was emotionally wound up and that he, Dick, was in the firing line. But he thought everyone had the right to get things off their chests, and he would not deny Harry that right. However, we had some business to attend to, and he slowly drew the meeting back to its proper starting point.

This incident provided me with a very useful way of managing an explosive situation.

tools. Personal observation can be a powerful way of learning, even when one is not personally *involved*. Consider the case on the previous page.

During this exchange I was only a bystander, an observer, albeit one with an interest in what was happening. Yet for me it was a very useful learning experience. I had sometimes wondered what I would do if someone lost their temper in a situation which I would have to handle, and Dick's measured and understanding response gave me a method for containing events. (It turned out, later, that Dick had had plenty of experience of dealing with explosions of this kind.) In passing, it is also worth pointing out some of the other characteristics of learning from experience; although it was many years ago, my *expectations* were confounded by Harry's behaviour, and *emotions* were roused, and later I realized that I had been provided with a useful technique.

Before leaving this discussion of our own observations, it is worthwhile repeating and re-enforcing the point made earlier in the chapter on opportunity regarding the advantages of writing about an experience. Jeff Gold and colleagues[1] stressed the value of an individual writing an account of an experience as a first part of the process of reflection. We have already seen in the opportunity chapter how writing helps to capture immediate impressions of, and quite possibly questions raised by, an experience, but Gold *et al.* make the point that the production of a text 'brings the past into the present'. Having jotted down what we saw, heard, felt, thought, believed, and so on, as soon as possible after an experience, it is then possible at a later date, maybe a few days afterwards, to read the text with more detachment than when we wrote it. It can then be looked at critically,[2] so that assumptions can be challenged: for example, 'would she see that comment in the same way as I did?', or 'is his motivation likely to be the same as other people's – or, at least, mine'? We can put on our 'sceptical spectacles' when we read, which will almost certainly lead to fuller and more objective insights.

FELLOW PARTICIPANTS' OBSERVATIONS

Dan, whose ability to learn from experience was so impressive that it was he, more than anyone else, who inspired me to research the subject, had an

---

1   Jeff Gold, Richard Thorpe and Robin Holt (2007) came up with the notion of 'the three Rs of manager learning'. (They were writing in the context of managers, but the principles seem universal.) These are writing, reading and reason, and they neatly span much of the rest of this book.

2   Michael Reynolds (1998) distinguishes between reflection and 'critical reflection'; the latter entails challenging assumptions, for example about cultural norms and social values.

interesting habit. Towards the end of a day after meetings we had both attended he would wander into my office and launch a conversation with questions such as: what do you think Joe was really getting at? Why did Mary react so strongly? and who did Jim have in mind when he said … ? My answers might be accepted or challenged, and sometimes they led to Dan putting forth a hypothesis which was verging on the absurd, clearly intended to provoke me into further reflection and comment.

This was far from idle chatter. When he walked in, Dan had some issues on his mind which he could not quite understand, which from his perspective did not make total sense, and the purposes of the questions and the hypotheses were to seek another perspective, to obtain more data.

It was no surprise, therefore, that when I came to research experiential learning by listening to people describe what their experiences had meant to them, the accounts I heard were very often examples of group learning – where the group could be two or more. Usually, when I asked my research colleague to describe his or her experience they did so in the first person – 'I did this' or 'I felt that' – but as we discussed how they had been able to make sense of the experience it frequently emerged that colleagues had contributed in some way. Thus Rick, mentioned in the introduction to this chapter, said almost in passing that he generally discussed matters with colleagues who were in the same boat, in the pub after work. The way Rick came to look at his predicament, that it was not a particularly personal experience, and the solution he worked out, that of moving to a client firm in New York, was clearly mediated to some degree and in some fashion by his chats in the pub.

Al volunteered the importance of colleagues. He said his favourite question was 'what do you think?', and he esteemed a former boss who used to open up reviews of past actions with the question 'how have I been wrong?'. This last question, incidentally, is particularly useful, even when there hadn't been much wrong; it entitled others, especially more junior people, to make whatever constructive comment they wished, without having to open up by saying to the boss that he was wrong.

It is not quite as simple, however, as going round asking lots of open questions of friends and colleagues. Karl Weick, a professor in organizational psychology, stresses the need for what he calls *respectful interaction*. He studied[3]

3   Weick (1993) based his study on a book by Norman Maclean called *Young Men and Fire*. Weick's own article is entitled 'The collapse of sense-making in organisations: the Mann Gulch disaster'.

a tragic incident in the US when a team of young firefighters were flown in to put out a forest fire and of the 15 in the team all but four perished. The team was spread out over a wide area, but two were able to work together to devise a strategy for escaping the oncoming fire; they saw a point on a ridge where they knew the fire-front would stop, and worked out the best route for reaching it before the fire did. By 'respectful interaction' Weick means that each should be an equal partner, his example being the two survivors. Each should value the other's contribution, and should also value their own contribution sufficiently highly to put it forward. Each of the two young men had sufficient self-confidence, and confidence in the other, to co-operate by pooling their knowledge and agreeing an optimal plan, which saved their lives.

The implications of respectful interaction are therefore a willingness both to speak and to listen. Dan was very good at both. After posing his question he sat back and listened intently, nodding or frowning as he agreed or disagreed, and then put his own point of view – which was clearly open to modification. Moreover, and this is a point Weick makes quite strongly, questions of hierarchy should not enter into the reckoning. Simply because A has a bigger job and is responsible for B does not mean, necessarily, that A's view is superior to B's. To a lesser extent, professional or technical expertise might, also, be suspended: when it comes to a matter of what someone saw or heard, other people, although less expert, may well be valuable in providing more observational data than the expert alone possesses.

So although Sartre (1947) said 'Hell is other people', salvation may also lie in the observations of others.

INFORMED NON-PARTICIPANTS' OBSERVATIONS

Other people could also be very helpful in making sense of an experience, even though they did not actually participate in it. Although they are non-participants, their questions or comments, that is their observations, could help in the learning process.

I described in the account above how the union official Dick had been very impressive in handling a potentially explosive meeting by responding to Harry's tirade of abuse with equanimity and good humour, and later I mentioned this to my boss. He was not as impressed as I was, and pointed out that Dick had had to face this kind of situation many times in shop-floor meetings, and had clearly worked out a way of responding to it. This aspect of Dick's background had not occurred to me, and while it did not diminish Dick's skill, my boss's comment helped to explain Dick's facility. So for me, in this learning situation, my boss was an 'informed non-participant' whose observations contributed to my learning. He had not been in the meeting, but when I described the incident to him he was able to understand, and account for, Dick's obvious ability.

Several of my interviewees spoke of the value of having access to someone who, although not directly involved in the events under discussion, was able to offer insights, by questioning or commenting, which served to clarify, focus, or even explain a confusing or problematic situation. Anne talked of a colleague who, during the early days of her time in an organization, had been someone who was extremely helpful in interpreting a wide variety of events so that she could better understand how the organization worked. During our discussion, Jim (having described his difficult meeting in Chapter 2) said 'I always like a buddy, someone I can meet after work to whom I can unload, and he can unload to me. It is very helpful – we can discuss how to react to difficult problems.' (You may remember this comment as an example in Chapter 6 of an *opportunity* for exploring an experience.)

There are several points to make about non-participants' observations. First, the ball is very much in your court, to play as you see fit. Anne did not *have* to initiate the discussions which led to helpful interpretations, and Jim did not *have* to have a buddy. I did not *have* to mention Dick's reaction to my boss – but in each case, the choice was made, and we learned as a result.

Two things underpin this. We each had to have a *network* of people to whom we could turn when events were puzzling or problematic. As it happens, for Anne, Jim and myself, our colleagues were in-house, but in other instances they could be well outside the organization. The crucial quality they had was the ability to understand the scene we were describing, probably because they had been there themselves, and use this knowledge to illuminate our problems. We each had to *trust* the non-participants, to know that whatever we say will be treated in confidence and not used to embarrass us or other people. Of course, trust works both ways; the non-participant has to trust us to use whatever learning arises with discretion – as Anne's colleague said – 'You usually have two chances, but if trust is abused after the second, then that's it.'

Paradoxically, some of the value of working with a non-participant lies in the requirement on ourselves to articulate clearly the scene we are finding problematic. Karl Weick quotes a little girl who said 'How can I know what I think until I see what I say?',[4] by which she meant that the process of taking

4   Weick's *Sensemaking in Organisations* (1995), page 12.

thoughts, which exist solely in her brain, and converting them into words, which she could speak (or write) and communicate to the outside world, that is beyond her own person, started her opportunity to make critical sense of what she thought. A more sophisticated person than a little girl would build in a judgement filter to separate out thoughts/words she felt might be unacceptable to the hearer, and save her from the embarrassment of blurting out a naive or hurtful statement, but the first part of the process is the same – that of articulating thoughts.

It is well known that the act of describing something helps to fix it in our minds, as noted earlier in the chapter on memory, and it also helps to clarify it. Most people want to 'speak sense', that is to say things, or write them, which are comprehensible to others, or alternatively and only if necessary, to preface their words with a phrase like 'I can't explain it, but…'.[5] So the first benefit of sense-making with a non-participant begins here.

What sort of a person would make a good informed non-participant? Essentially, there are two qualities: experience and acceptability. Obviously, you would want someone who is familiar with the type of event or incident which you need to explore, or at least whose knowledge and understanding of the world suggests that they would readily understand your experience. I was once struggling to come to terms with my failure to deliver a training programme in an organization, and related it to Joe, a friend who was also a part-time colleague; he had not worked in that organization, but said that others of its type were often reluctant receivers of training, because they believed they knew it all already(!), but in any case I had probably been over-ambitious by starting with 'systems theory', one of the more difficult elements of the programme. He would have brought it in much later when he had a better idea of the strengths of personnel, and knew better how to present it. Joe was an excellent person to help me understand my failure, because he knew the kind of organization and the dynamics that could prevail, and he also knew the type of subject matter I had been asked to present. He was a highly informed non-participant.

Joe also had the other quality that is important, namely acceptability. He was someone with whom I felt at ease talking about almost anything. He was a good listener, not judgemental but not afraid to say where he thought I might have been over-ambitious, or where my emotions could cloud my judgement.

---

5   For example, Cortese, in an article on learning through teaching, says 'The recounting of stories aloud in front of a third person, intent on bringing out and stimulating the memory of facts and persons, provided an almost unique opportunity for the re-appropriation of the learning experience matured through the work life, and which in some cases had been forgotten' (2005) page 110.

The benefits of discussing experiences, especially with an informed non-participant in a safe environment, have been recognized by several writers, perhaps most notably by Kolb and colleagues.[6] Building on the model of experiential learning (Figure 2.1) they observe that the articulation of ideas, thoughts, queries and feelings are helpful as 'a process whereby learners construct meaning and transform experiences into knowledge through conversation'. For them, conversational learning can be structured around five dialectic poles. (Dialectics, according to *Chambers Dictionary*, is 'the art of discussing, especially a debate which seeks to resolve the conflict between two opposing theories, rather than disprove any one of them'.) The five poles are:

1. *Apprehension*, feelings oriented, v. *comprehension*, reason-oriented

2. *Intension*, contemplation and reflection, v. *extension*, experimentation

3. *Individuality*, the self, v. *relationality*, connection with others

4. *Status*, position within a group, v. *solidarity*, equality within it

5. *Discursive orientation*, guided by linear time, v. *recursive orientation*, cyclical time.

Clearly, an individual might feel pulled both ways within any one, or indeed all five, of these poles, but the surfacing of such thoughts in order to share them with others, and the listening to others' comparable comments and observations, could well be of real value in 'constructing meaning and transforming experiences into knowledge'. In my discussion with Joe about my unhappy experience with the training programme, for example, on the apprehension/comprehension pole I had feelings of annoyance and mild despair at having failed, which were rubbing up against the belief that I was doing the rights things for the course – and doing them reasonably well. Joe's empathetic listening, and then his comments on what I was trying to do in the context of my clients, certainly helped in my understanding of how things had gone wrong and what would have been a better method of approach.

Finally, the informed non-participant is someone who, if shown a text of the type advocated by Gold *et al.* in the paragraphs above on our *own observations*, would probably be in a good position to help challenge your underlying assumptions. What might seem an obvious cause and effect to you could well

---

6   Baker, Jensen and Kolb (2002). An example of this approach is given in an article by Anna B Kayes (2007).

be revealed as something far less automatic, and therefore offer the possibility of much truer learning. The fact that it was written at the time means that they could work with a clean, first-hand account, free of later accretions of interpretation.

LINKED OBSERVATIONS

I hope that the foregoing sections have given some idea of the variety of contributions, and some of their distinctive natures, that can be made by other people to fill out and amplify the data which we observe for ourselves of an experience. However, as I said in the introduction, it would be a mistake to view them as discrete and separable. Although we generally start with our own observations, they are open to modification and amplification, as a result of what other people in the same experience have seen, and possibly to comments from an informed non-participant.

For example, when Rick was being eased out of his City finance job he found real advantage from discussing what was happening to him with his colleagues, who were suffering the same fate. After broaching the subject tentatively, to check whether people were meeting the same problem, once he had heard that others were in the same boat he would have borne in mind their ideas as he formulated his own. The big issue they all faced was that of 'fight or flight?' Listening to others he concluded that *fight*, that is opposing the new owner's intention of clearing out the layer of staff that included him, was futile, that he would lose, and that his energies were better devoted to developing a productive *flight* plan. As he did this, again he heard colleagues talking about their possibilities, and Rick's own plan bore some resemblance to others, and in fact of the group affected, two others, like Rick, found comparable – and better – jobs in New York finance firms. So although it was a highly personal experience for Rick, the way he dealt with it was influenced to quite a large extent by how his fellows were seeing it.

The point, of course, is that as events in his firm unfolded over several weeks, Rick's perception of what was happening was influenced by his colleagues, and the lessons he learned from the experience were almost certainly modified in some way by their observations. Thus after the first meeting in the pub after work, he began to see what was happening as more the need for the new owner to stamp his mark on the firm than a belief that Rick was in some measure inadequate. What was happening to him was structural rather than personal. As it happened, Rick did not have access to an informed non-participant who could have helped through such a traumatic time, but had such a person been available the outcome might have been very similar. Whatever the reality, it brings me to the second point, namely the significance of *time*.

Rick made his own observations and heard his colleagues' views over the period of several weeks, during which time his thoughts and emotions would have changed and developed. Jim, who in the previous section was quoted as saying 'I always like a buddy', was describing his preference over a long period, probably measured in many months or years, rather than a one-off occasion. So at one meeting, Jim would have mentioned some experience currently on his mind and his buddy would have made (generally) insightful comments; at the next meeting, the buddy could very well have added to them, while Jim might have had further thoughts, perhaps prompted by the buddy's initial observations. What Jim valued was the opportunity for an ongoing dialogue, towards the end of which, with helpful comments from his buddy, he could have taken appropriate action and learned some lessons.

POINTS FOR EXPLORATION

This section is about data-gathering – the acquisition of information about an experience – from which we hope to be able to make some sense and learn some lessons. This chapter focuses on our involvement with an experience and the several ways in which we can gather more facts and ideas from ourselves, from others who were in the same experience, and from those who were not there but could understand it. So some questions to ponder for ourselves include:

- What can we remember about the experience, using Kipling's 'honest serving men' questions, (what, where, when, how, why, and who), and also, possibly, which?

- To help fill out this recollection, can we write it down, or at least tell someone about it in some detail?

    (i) was there anyone else in the same experience whose perception of it we can seek? Who could add, or possibly challenge what we had seen?

- Is there an informed non-participant who is able to throw light on it by actually explaining it, or by asking questions lead us to possible explanations, and who can do this in an acceptable manner?

(i)   when looking back, especially if we have a written account of an experience, how critical can we be by challenging assumptions and beliefs? Can an informed non-participant help in this process?

CHAPTER 10

Formal Knowledge and Our Own Experience

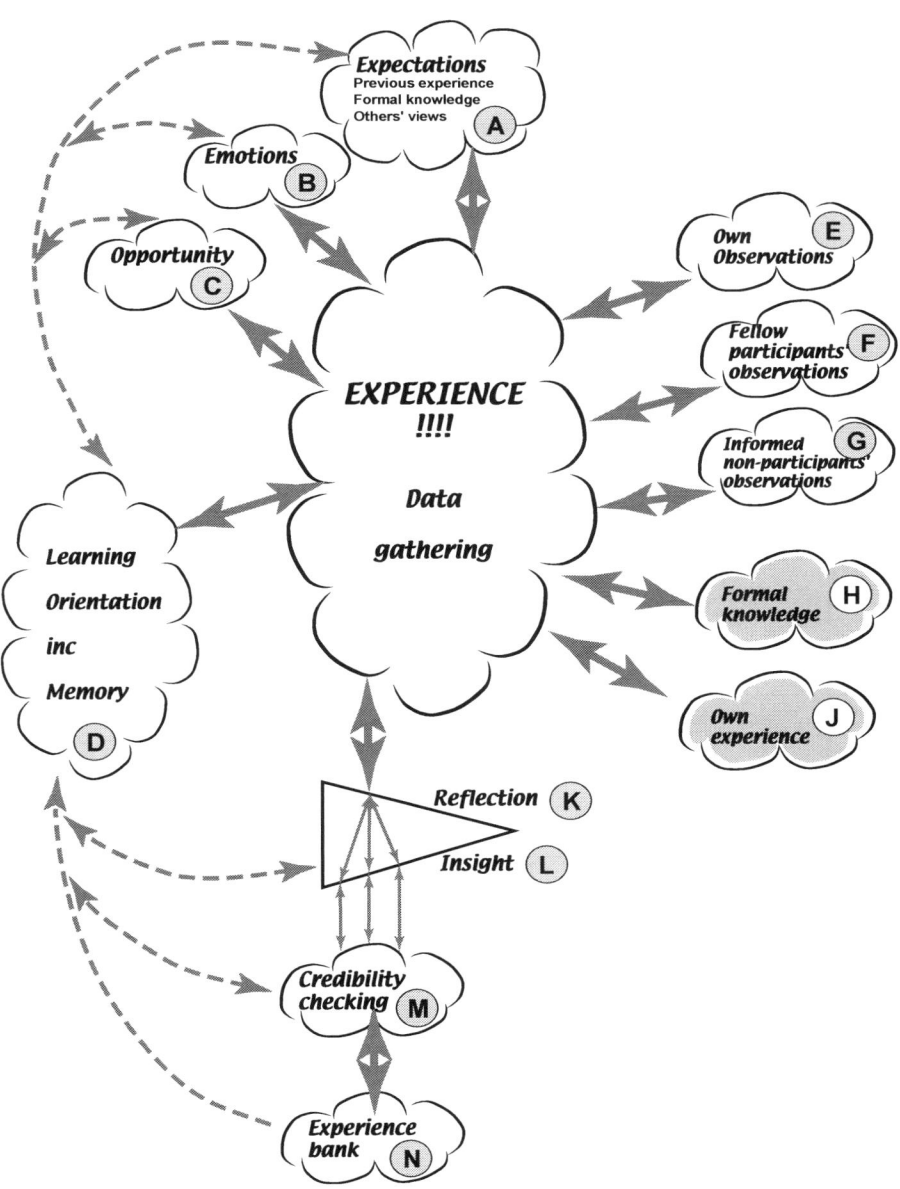

INTRODUCTION

The previous chapter looked at how we acquire information about an experience from current, live sources, namely what we perceive ourselves, what other people in the same experience can offer and what can be suggested by someone who understands this kind of experience. As we start to think about *this* experience, these are the people from whom we can hope to gather most data.

However, this experience may well resemble other events which have occurred in the past and about which there may be some, a little or a lot, information in the public domain, which may be helpful in enabling us to make sense of the experience. In Chapter 3, I related my experience with the time-expired grass seed which did not germinate, adding that it was only when I recalled an article on the shelf-lives of different types of seed that my problem became clear. The data on seed viability, which solved the problem, was in the public domain, namely a newspaper article on gardening, and, no doubt, in the appropriate horticultural research journals should I wish to follow it up.

Formal knowledge in the public domain seems an incontrovertible element in our overall sense-making, but why bracket it with our *own experience* in this chapter, even though it seems equally relevant as an independent element? The answer lies in our capacity to internalize formal knowledge, shape it for our own needs, and make it our own. At this point it becomes so personalized that we tend to forget that our understanding of it started 'out there', in the public domain, in a textbook, a lecture or a demonstration.

A question I have often asked professional people is: How much of the knowledge and skill that you use to do your normal work is based on experience, and, by contrast, how much on textbooks, lectures, journals and so on? The answers typically range from 60–80 per cent from experience and the balance from formal knowledge. Yet these are professional people whose basic knowledge of theory and technique was gained from many years' study; they could not practice their professions without the grounding they received as young adults, which shaped their whole approach to their subsequent work. But now, often two or more decades after their official training finished, the theory and technique acquired early in life is overlooked, they recall the experiences which have confirmed the theory and polished their technique, and attribute the greater part of their ability to do their work to 'experience'.

In their state of 'unconscious competence'[1] they probably overlook the effort needed to get there.

So because formal knowledge merges, in time and with use, into our own experience, it seems preferable to treat them together.

FORMAL KNOWLEDGE

As described above, formal knowledge is information which already exists in the public domain, available, at least in theory, to everyone. It includes virtually all the academic material that students learn in school, in occupational/ vocational courses, universities, professional training courses, in-house courses, night schools and so on. It also includes the material that we read in books, magazines, journals, on the web and in newspapers, together with what we see on TV, posters and even graffiti, and what we hear on the radio, from friends and colleagues, and overhear in public places.

The unifying characteristic of all this knowledge is that it has been presented, and in some cases created, by someone 'out there', writing or speaking on subjects that are of their choice. Someone else has chosen to write texts, decided what to include in courses, what to say on air and in person. Much the greatest part of it that we use in sense-making is formal, although it shades into the informal when it includes gossip and graffiti.

Sharp readers will be saying: if it includes what we hear from friends and colleagues, does it not overlap the observations made by *fellow participants* and *informed non-participants*, as discussed in the previous chapter? The answer is: well yes, in a sense, but the distinction relates to the question choice. In the *formal knowledge* that we use to help us learn, we resort to information *others* have prepared for general consumption, whereas in the *fellow participants' observations*, and the *informed non-participants' observations*, *we* have actively sought the comments of others, tailored to the experience in question.

When I was carrying out my research into how people learn from experience, most people made little reference to formal knowledge, perhaps because they had internalized much of it, but those that did evinced a wide variety of sources.

---

1   The four stages of learning are sometimes described as *unconscious incompetence*, when you don't know that you can't do something, *conscious incompetence*, you recognize you have much to learn, *conscious competence*, when you have learned to do something but it requires your full attention, and *unconscious competence*, when an activity becomes so much part of second nature that it can be done with hardly any attention. For many people, learning to drive a car illustrates this sequence.

Anne, for example, whose strong academic background was recognized by her informal mentor, received articles and books when she sought explanations of events from her mentor. She said:

> I think the learning process was partly academic. It was being given tracts that said 'here is another way to do this', the theory, and because of my educational background, theory appeals to me, theories and principles you can use to understand what is going on.

Keith quoted a business course he had followed as being invaluable in illuminating some of the activities in his organization; he referred to 'the languages of different disciplines', and the insights and understandings they gave him. Tim had read about a particular technique for looking at a whole organization, and the various systems that are working within that organization, which, once he had grasped the approach, proved invaluable whenever he encountered a new company or business, or a major part of one. Vince, a senior executive responsible for strategic development, said:

> Learning at the top level is very much about awareness, what is really happening in the market place. What is the FT saying today? What are commentators saying? What are other companies doing in their strategic developments? What are the benchmark companies doing? Learning, in the sense of day-to-day learning, is an accumulation of a framework in which you are trying place your own company.

Dan pointed to the potential of *people* as sources of formal knowledge. He described how, with a law qualification and extensive experience of different functions in his company, he was given line responsibility for technical operations. He found that the quickest and most efficient way of learning was to work with selected members of his staff, and, taking specific examples, explore the theory and practice within which the examples were located. So with person A, whose background and experience was in chemistry, he would look at the work of a chemical processing department, at the theory of the individual processes, and the practical matters that influenced the day-to-day running of the department. Person B would provide comparable information in, say, mechanical engineering, and so on. Dan's source of formal knowledge lay in the people who worked with him, and he used a questioning technique (Kipling's questions, again) to help him understand the issues his company was facing. Of course, he was dependent, at least in the early stages, on the quality and integrity of his 'tutors', but he was very skilled at working with people, at motivating them and enabling them to contribute to the greatest possible extent.

Some experiences may be beyond the scope of *current* formal knowledge. For example, in the text below there is a brief account of the investigation which followed two disastrous crashes of the Comet jet plane. At the time of the incidents, after sabotage and pilot error had been ruled out, there was no explicable cause for the crashes, that is to say that formal knowledge, as it currently existed, could offer no reasons. The investigation carried out by the RAE at Farnborough added to formal knowledge, so that today, in cases of the collapse of metal structures, the possibility of metal fatigue as a contributory cause would be automatically considered. Researchers, and practitioners in general, are constantly perusing professional journals in their fields so that they can keep abreast on formal knowledge, as it is constantly being added to, challenged and discussed.

Research into the Comet Aircraft Crashes*
Metal Fatigue Caused Comet Crashes

In 1954, two years after it came into service, the Comet jet airliner, the first commercial jet in the world, had its certificate of airworthiness withdrawn after two crashes resulting in the deaths of 56 people.

An exhaustive investigation was carried out by the Royal Aircraft Establishment at Farnborough. Thousands of fragments of the second plane were recovered from the sea near Elba, and models and full-size aircraft were subjected to rigorous testing.

One fragment showed that a crack had developed due to metal fatigue at the corner of a window, and tests showed that such a small weakness would quickly deteriorate under pressure, leading to the sudden and general break-up of the fuselage.

The plane's windows were re-designed from rectangular to round, and the Comet 4 continued in service into the 1980s.

* This summary is based on a text in the BBC series *On This Day* for 19 October, accessible on the web.

OWN EXPERIENCE

This is the last of the elements grouped under the heading of data gathering, and it is in this sense that it is discussed below. It has obvious connections with other elements. It links with *expectations* when an experience comes along which contrasts in some way with our own experience. In Chapter 9, I described how my expectations of Harry in a formal negotiating meeting were totally confounded when he opened up with a rude and abusive tirade against his union colleagues. It links with *memory*, because our own experience has no value if we are unable to recall similar or related experiences – as for the unfortunate musician Clive Wearing mentioned in Chapter 8. It also has links with *learning orientation*; our personalities, and specifically our openness to the possibility of new connections, influences how we view an experience, and our ability to register detail depends on our ability in the relevant intelligence.

For all these reasons, our own experience is a highly personal element in experiential learning, changing as we age, acquiring new facts and ways of looking at things as we live our lives, but liable to erosion or diminution as we forget. It is also linked with the major element of *reflection/insight* in so far as we often start with our own experiences when we are seeking to make sense of a new experience, and learn from it.

I said in the introduction to this chapter that as time passes and we use formal knowledge it often becomes subsumed into own our experience. In the box below is an account of how a technique, first encountered in a textbook

---

Tanya's Experience of Measuring Blood Pressure

Tanya had had a rapid rise in her nursing career. From enrolling as a student nurse to becoming the Senior Sister in the stroke ward of a busy teaching hospital had taken only a few years, during which time many basic nursing practices had become firmly established. She described, as an example, the measurement of blood pressure.

'As student nurses we had classroom training in understanding the theory of blood pressure and the technique of measuring it. From a standard text [Brunner and Suddarth 1989] we would practice on each other, finding it very difficult not only to understand the implications of changes in blood pressure but even measuring it in all but the simplest cases. Over the years, using the technique with many different types of patient in a variety of different medical situations, I gradually became familiar with it and confident in its use.

Now its use is almost second nature. Even a short glance tells me whether a patient's condition merits measurement of blood pressure, and my interpretation of the result leads me to the exercise of discretion in the administration of normal drugs, as prescribed by the Consultant. It's surprising, and reassuring, how an understanding of some principles and plenty of practice make something become a natural part of me!'

and on a training course, became so personalized as to be part of the normal repertoire of a professional.

Thus for Tanya, the *formal knowledge* contained in a standard nursing textbook, supplemented by practice in formal training sessions, was used and practised over the years to a point where it became part of her second nature, part of the repertoire of a successful and highly competent professional.

Our own experience is often, perhaps usually, quite consciously used to learn from a new experience. One of my research colleagues, Garry, had a background in company finance and extensive experience of working with line colleagues on various financial matters in the UK and Holland, when he went on a visit to a newly acquired subsidiary in the United States. His image of America, formed from films, TV, and reputations created by gurus of all sorts, a sort of vicarious own experience, led him to expect, as he put it, 'the cutting edge, the [financial] systems will be great, they'll be knowing what they're doing'. Yet what he found was very much like home: 'they're just a small company, with the same problems as everyone else'. So starting with his own experience, Garry had expected to learn one type of lesson, to do with slick systems and advanced techniques, and yet he actually learned a very different lesson: 'problems are identical the world over, things we come across here are hardly any different from what everyone else struggles with everywhere' . Garry is too wise to generalize from one experience, but that one experience was enough to shake his, he would say somewhat naive, belief in the supremacy of the US.

It is worth noting that our own experience broadly encompasses *facts/ beliefs* and *methods*. Facts include hard data, such as that the earth is a planet, impressions – that my colleague is liable to lose his temper rather easily – and ideas or beliefs – that 'capitalism' has some national characteristics. We use these daily to inform our actions, to decide which route to follow to work (if we drive), to add to our store of interesting/useful information on a subject of general interest, to challenge new 'facts' which are apparently in conflict with those we already hold to be true, to take decisions of all sorts.

Methods are different, in that they are concerned with procedures, ways of doing things or approaching problems. They can be literally 'hands-on', for example the method for baking a cake, have a specific end point such as the planning of a party, or be entirely conceptual, the way of looking at complex organisms or problems. An example of the way of looking at things was given earlier in the section on formal knowledge, namely that of Tim who was introduced to 'systems thinking' when engaged on a project: he found it so useful in understanding the relationships between different parts of his part of his company that he was able to internalize it and use it in quite different settings, when he was working with a large number of different companies in a major national industry, for example.

The American educationalist Donald Schön, in his book *The Reflective Practitioner*, makes the point that professionals of all kinds draw on their own experience continuously. He refers to the practice of 'recourse to repertoire' as part of the process of 'reflection-in-action', where the repertoire includes 'examples, images, understandings, and actions'.[2] So an architect, one of Schön's examples, designing a school on a new and difficult site, continuously refers back in his mind to other work he has done or has studied, drawing on techniques which could be considered for the present building. Schön refers to it as a 'dialogue with the problem', in which the architect is almost literally saying to the problem 'well how about trying this solution: what do you think of that?', and listening to, that is to say judging, the response.

Another illustration of methods of approach, of a way of looking at things, from my own experience is that of paying attention to *context* when looking at human situations. The importance of context struck me early in my professional career when I observed that a certain union colleague could behave very differently on different occasions, and I was puzzled by this varied behaviour. Some variations were easy to discern, as when he was rather boisterous when meeting me in the afternoon, straight from the pub! Others took more fathoming, but I found that the greeting 'How are you? What's on your mind today?' was usually enough to give me a clear indication of his frame of mind. When I knew his prevailing attitude I could judge the weight of what he had to say, how to respond, and how and when to launch any initiatives I had in mind.

Judging contexts, it seems to me, is an important part of working in almost any human situation. The new coach of a football team would probably behave quite differently with a team which had a long run of losses compared with one with a winning record; a tutor would adopt a different approach for an advanced pupil as compared with a beginner; a supervisor would, hopefully, handle the problems of a recently bereaved member of staff more sympathetically than

---

2   Schön (1983) page 138. Schön goes on to quote Thomas Kuhn, who coined the term 'paradigm shift' for very major changes in ways of looking at things, as saying 'confronted with a problem, [one] seeks to see it as like one or more of the exemplary problems he has encountered before …' (page 139).

normal and so on. Once the significance of context is recognized, appropriate action can be taken.

Dan illustrated this well when he described his dilemma when appointed to a top line post. The world of line management, as he perceived it, was pretty directive, with instructions and directions being issued quite tersely and without any dressing up. As such, it contrasted with his experience of senior functional management, in which explanation and persuasion were key elements. He said:

> *I had to learn whether everything that had been appropriate to manoeuvrings and so on that had been effective in a staff [functional] position were still appropriate to a line position. I think that in the end I came, again through trial and error, to the conclusion that they probably were. If you come up the line route there is a bit more of 'bang-bang' about it, but if you come up a route in which you've had to manoeuvre and shift to make things happen all the way, in a way I think it helps you to bring that to line positions, because you don't just go 'bang-bang', you still try and make it by consensus.*

So here Dan was drawing on his own experience in one context and testing it in another. In Schön's phrase, he was having recourse to his repertoire of techniques for getting things done.

It will be apparent that in these examples of gathering data from our own experience, I have moved on into the next part of experiential learning or sense-making, namely the element of *reflection and insight* – the subject of the next chapter. *Reflection and insight* is not a discrete element that only clicks in when all the data from an experience has been gathered. Rather, it permeates our own experience, challenging the data already provided. For example, of a piece of *formal knowledge*, it might say 'can I believe that – I've never heard of that before!', or of a *fellow participant's observations* it might say 'that is a very different account from my own: can I trust it?', or indeed of one's *own observation*, it might say 'did I *really* see or hear that?'

In a sense, therefore, our own experience seems to be transitory between the straightforward data-gathering activities of the other elements and the more thinking, evaluating and concluding activities of reflection and insight. On balance, however, and with an eye to keeping the Model of experiential learning as simple as possible, it has seemed preferable to retain it with the data-gathering elements because, for many experiences, it counts as a major provider.

POINTS FOR EXPLORATION

FORMAL KNOWLEDGE

- It would be interesting to look back on some recent experiences and see where your formal sources of information were – books, school/ university course, newspapers, radio, TV and so on.

- For one or two facts/beliefs that are part of your work repertoire, how much is derived from formal knowledge, acquired, for example, quite early in your development in the vocation? And how has that original contribution been enhanced and built up through your subsequent experience?

OUR OWN EXPERIENCE

- As for formal knowledge, in recent experiences – how much, and in what ways, did your own experience contribute?

- When you use your own experience, how was that developed in the first place?

CHAPTER 11

Reflection and Insight

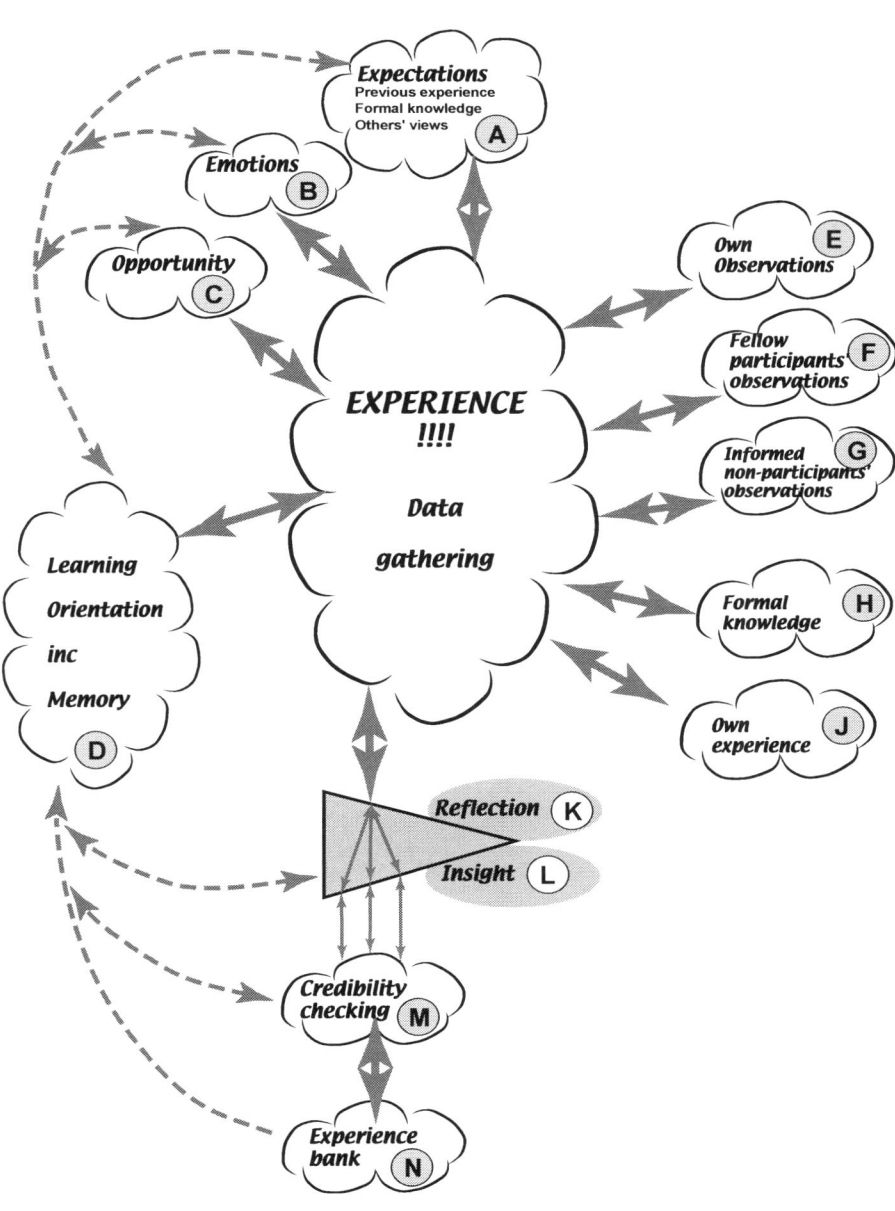

INTRODUCTION

Finally, we come to the core process of learning from experience, that of making sense of as much as possible of what we have seen, heard, felt and so on. If the experience is at all complex, to arrive at this phase we have, probably, (i) had our *expectations* challenged, and (ii) our *emotions* roused sufficiently to spend time and energy in exploring the experience, (iii) taken whatever *opportunities* we have to dig into it, (iv) applied our own, unique *learning orientation* to approach it, (v) checked out our *own observations*, together with (vi) those of *fellow participants*, and (vii) *informed non-participants*, perhaps consulted (viii) any source of *formal knowledge* that seemed applicable, and (ix) our *own experience* – all this to prepare ourselves for the crucial process of reflecting on the experience with a view to learning whatever lessons it has to offer.

Very possibly most of this has been unconscious. Certainly, it is very unlikely that as part of our preparation we have reviewed our own personality, and pretty unlikely that our emotions have remained unchanged throughout. For some experiences, all the above elements may seem to constitute a ponderous sledgehammer poised over a very small nut; the pain felt from touching something hot, for example, tells me that in future I must not do it again, an insight arrived at in milliseconds.

Yet even for such a short experience, most of the elements are clearly relevant. For more complex experiences there can be many lessons to learn, some of which are learnt quickly while others can take days, weeks, or even years. A colleague and I interviewed Ian, a senior engineer in the water industry who had had the experience of dealing with a very major incident when a burst water main had led to the loss of clean water for half a big city, about a quarter of a million people.[1] Ian described several very different strands of learning from the disaster, ranging from the metallurgy of the water main, and the problems of shutting down such a large diameter pipe (42"), through the relationships with nearby householders whose properties had been flooded, to the psychology of his work colleagues whose efforts over the period of a week had been superb. Not only were these just a few of several major lessons he had learnt, but the time taken to learn them varied greatly from a few hours to many months. Indeed, there were some issues which still puzzled him 18 years after the event.

---

1   An account of the incident, and how this model of learning from experience could be applied to the engineer's learning, is given by Davies and Kraus (2003) in Chapter 12 of *HRD in a Complex World* (2003), edited by Monica Lee.

This possible complexity of sorting out the different types of lesson to be learnt from an experience led me to the notion of representing this element as a prism, rather than the amorphous cloud-like shapes used for all other elements. Just as a prism separates out a beam of white light into its component colours, the reflection and insight element of the Model allows for a complex experience, possibly lasting a long time, teasing out its disparate components, making their various lessons more easily comprehensible. However, like all the other elements, the arrows are two-way. As Ian, in the example above, pondered, for example, the metallurgy of the water main, his first thoughts, and probably his second and third thoughts, failed at the *credibility checking* stage, and he returned to seek more data from colleagues, including *informed non-participants*, and his *own experience*. Indeed, it was only after exhaustive tests by the relevant Research Association, that is by the production of *formal knowledge*, that he was able to understand the likely cause of the problem – a flaw in the wall of the pipe, probably caused at the time of the pipeline construction in the late nineteenth century. These iterations between different elements illustrate the possibly complex nature of sense-making and learning.

It is worth noting at this stage the wisdom of a comment by Francis Crick, the discoverer, with Jim Watson, of the double-helix structure of DNA. He said that 'a theory that fits all the facts is bound to be wrong, as some of the facts will be wrong'! (This is presumably a 'first pass' comment, that is to say it relates to the first set of data, the first facts that are produced. With refinement, we must hope that fewer and fewer facts will be wrong.) The implication of the remark is to encourage us to stay with our early thoughts or hypotheses for a while, even though they may seem not to fit the facts. Only when the facts appear to be really solid and incontrovertible is it time to go firm on, or rethink, the ideas.

Incidentally, Francis Crick was a well-known user of the collaborative approach to research, for whom the term 'respectful interaction', which we met in *fellow participants' observations*, would have been a watch-word. In his work with Watson and other scientists, he would be utterly candid without being rude, and had a rule of everyone being able to say whatever came into their heads without fear of criticism. This encouraged the sharing of ideas, however half-formed, and ensured that no concept was strangled at birth.

Returning to the element of reflection and insight, because it is such a broad subject we will deal with it under the 'input–process–output' model, which for our purposes I am calling Prompts, Process, and Products.

PROMPTS

We have already met the prompts, or as some writers call them, cues, for sense-making and learning, in Chapters 4 and 5 on *expectations* and *emotions*. When we looked at expectations, we saw that while we are normally in the default mode, that is we expect things will be as they have been in the past, we may be pulled out of this mode by something which is novel, or which is 'discrepant', that is contrasts with the norm, or by having our attention drawn to something of which we had hitherto been unaware.

Many of the examples in the boxes in earlier chapters illustrate these prompts. Thus in Jeannie's failure to face an old friend who was recently bereaved, in Jim's inability to deal with the cogent arguments of his union colleagues, in my puzzling over grass seed that did not grow, all contain some degree of mental unease caused by things being not what we thought they should be, that is they are 'discrepant'. In Chapter 4, Harry Brearley was struck by the steel which did not rust, a novelty which led to the development of the stainless steel industry, and in Chapter 10, the researchers into the Comet aircraft disasters were carrying out their tests into metal fatigue at the direction of the coroner and the request of the plane manufacturer.

Some prompts cause what one writer[2] on adult learning calls a 'disorientation' – literally a disturbance in the way we are facing, the way we see things. They may lead to changes in 'meaning schemes', specific subjects such as facts, day-to-day beliefs or judgements, or they may lead (less often) to changes in 'meaning perspectives', our fundamental beliefs created by ideologies and long experience. Naturally, changes in the latter are relatively rare, while changes in meaning schemes probably diminish gradually as we grow older and encounter less that is novel or discrepant.

Emotions, too, as we saw in Chapter 5, play a part both in drawing our attention to experiences in the first place, and in keeping us focused to work on them thereafter. Jeannie and Jim both felt disturbed, even humiliated, by their inability to handle the situations they described. Irritation prompted me to consider why my grass seed had not germinated, and curiosity drove Harry Brearley to explore the nature of the steel that did not rust. When I look back on the accounts of learning given by the people whose experiences provided the

---

2   Jack Mezirow, in *Transformative Dimensions of Adult Learning* quotes Ross Keane as describing the start of a major change in the way he saw life: 'a disorientation, an inner dis-equilibrium in which the harmony of the self is disturbed yet the problem is neither understood nor satisfactorily named' (1991), page 177.

primary research for my thesis, every one could point to an emotion of some sort which drove them towards understanding.

These prompts in themselves were not enough to sustain them in the subsequent work needed to pull out the lessons that were there to be learned, however. The elements of *opportunity* and *learning orientation*, including *memory*, came into play, ensuring that, in these examples at least, answers were found and lessons learned. I have known people who, less sensitive than Jeannie and Jim to their respective tribulations, would have shrugged their shoulders and walked away, without admitting the existence of any problem. They would have foregone the opportunity to learn. It is very possible that other workers in Brearley's steel works would have noticed that certain steels did not rust, but the fact would not have interested them as it did Brearley. The point here is, of course, that Jeannie, Jim, and Brearley had learning orientations which encouraged, even impelled, them to engage with their issues. They had personalities which were open to new thinking, willing, indeed wanting, to take on board new ideas: for Jeannie and Jim, new ways of behaving, for Brearley ways of developing a new product.

The prompts in these examples were also received by able, developed minds. All were mature in their jobs, with several years' experience to shape and build up their ways of perceiving new events or occurrences. Had the incidents described taken place much earlier in their careers it is quite possible that they would have registered less impact, and thus not been grabbed as events needing to be worked on. Different emotions drove them to make opportunities for this work, the sense of shame and inadequacy for Jeannie and Jim, and curiosity for Harry Brearley. Almost needless to say, without their capacity for memory, their efforts would have been futile.

So if the prompt section of this chapter is quite short, it is because much of the earlier part of the book leads up to it. Given the various types of prompt, and the data which is gathered from the various sources in Chapters 9 and 10, we are now in a position to explore some of the ways in which this information is worked on.

PROCESSES

By 'processes' I mean the various ways in which one experience, an incident or an event, can be converted into lessons or generalizations which we can then use to guide or inform our future actions or thinking.

The human brain seems to have an inbuilt need to understand and explain things. Early peoples encountering a total eclipse, for example, sought an explanation in terms of the feelings and actions of their gods; they rationalized that the gods were displeased with their behaviour in some way, and that the temporary removal of light was a warning that they should change. Indeed, for most of man's life on earth, many civilizations constructed quite sophisticated deity systems to whom they could ascribe the good and bad events in human life – fecundity, bountiful nature and noble spirits on the one side, and disasters, tribulations and evil on the other.

Generally speaking, more attention seemed to be paid to the adverse experiences, with the beneficial, hoped-for events being accepted with less attention. Although the importance of keeping the gods in good spirits was recognized, to ensure the hoped-for normality, much attention was paid to warding off evil spirits. This preoccupation with disasters and the events and objects that frighten us has two facets which lead to learning; one, the need to make sense of them, we will discuss below, while the other addresses a more fundamental part of our make-ups. The Harvard sociobiologist Edward O. Wilson (1978) put it thus:

> We're not just afraid of predators, we're transfixed by them, prone to weave stories and chatter endlessly about them, because fascination creates preparedness, and preparedness, survival. In a deeply tribal sense, we love our monsters.

Thus for primitive man, the awful fascination with, say, lions ensured that lions were kept in focus, and ways of avoiding them discussed and planned – which, as Wilson observes, helped to ensure that losses to lions were reduced. Less obvious hazards such as poor food hygiene were not known or understood, and therefore not tackled, although it is interesting to note that today, when promoting the importance of good hygiene, germs are often portrayed as little monsters!

The existence of two things which contradict each other, which clash or grate, as when the sun in a clear sky suddenly disappears during the daytime, or, in Jim's experience, arguments which he found entirely satisfactory were reasonably rubbished by his union colleagues, is sometimes referred to as a *dissonance*. It is a term used in music to describe two notes sounding together which are distinctly *un*harmonic, that is a discord. By extension, in normal speech it implies a disagreement, and when that disagreement or clash exists in one's mind, it is called *cognitive* dissonance.

The psychologist Leon Festinger studied cognitive dissonance and came up with some principles to describe it.[3] Basically, he said, the existence of dissonance causes pressure to reduce it, and the greater the dissonance, the greater the pressure. The results of this pressure include changes in behaviour, changes in cognition – that is what we believe and the way we see things – and a guarded willingness to embrace new information and opinions. So returning to our examples of Jeannie, Jim and Harry Brearley, the cognitive dissonance which Jeannie felt was that of her total inadequacy in facing up to her bereaved friend, a feeling that was so strong (the dissonance exerted a great pressure), that she determined to explore and practice ways of handling this kind of situation. Jim's dissonance was the realization that his arguments were failing to carry the day, and his sense of inadequacy (pressure of dissonance) was sufficiently great to make him rethink his approach and develop a new way of preparing for this type of meeting. Brearley's dissonance was more cerebral as he noticed the strange properties of the steel which did not rust, but he was probably a naturally curious man and the amazing quality of this particular steel, which was unlike every other example he had ever seen, was sufficiently distinctive to lead him to pursue his researches.

It is important to note that Festinger's theory of cognitive dissonance is one of *reduction* rather than removal. As we grow from infancy we learn to live with innumerable little contradictions and paradoxes, and as adults we recognize that the world is full of minor imperfections, as we see them, but that the struggle to iron out all the wrinkles is not worth the effort. So Festinger saw dissonance being reduced to a level which was cognitively acceptable. In Jeannie's case, she came to view her way of dealing with bereavement as being satisfactory, if not quite perfect; it meant that she could contemplate meeting and relating to bereaved people with a sufficient confidence that would leave her feeling reasonably relaxed about the encounter. Similarly, Jim's strategy for anticipating what would be in the minds of his audience, backed up by a basic understanding of their circumstances, led him to develop ways of preparing for meetings which generally achieved his desired results. (If they had not, the pressure for dissonance reduction would continue to be unacceptably great, and he would have continued to seek improvements.)

While the theory of cognitive dissonance reduction helps to explain *why* we seek to make sense of experiences, it does not attempt to say *how* this can be done, which is not at all surprising, given the very wide of experiences we encounter. During the course of my research several different ways of seeking explanations emerged and they are discussed below, but it is important to

---

3   Festinger (1957).

register at the outset that they are almost certainly not comprehensive. The six ways of sense-making are as follows.

HOW WE MAKE SENSE 1: EXPLANATIONS THROUGH LOGIC AND REASONING[4]

The application of logic to problems is an attractive way of working out, of learning, the lessons of experience in so far as it can be explained to others, critiqued and defended. Moreover, in most scientific and technical work various processes of logic are used to produce knowledge and conclusions; thus in the example of the Comet disasters, the researchers carried out many tests on the strength of the materials of the fuselage before concluding that metal fatigue around the windows caused decompression and hence the crash of the aircraft.

There are two types of logical reasoning – *induction* and *deduction*. Inductive reasoning draws generalized conclusions from particular instances or premises. Thus:

- The ball is wood, and it floats;

- The cube is wood, and it floats

- Therefore, wooden things float.

Deductive reasoning, on the other hand, starts with a general statement and infers conclusions from it. Thus if we accept the above conclusion, we could say:

- Wooden things float;

- The toy fish is wooden;

- Therefore, the toy fish should float.

From the point of view of learning from experience, as indeed in the realm of pure logic, however, there are real problems in relying on these forms of reasoning. For example, the *inductive* conclusion that 'wooden things float', while true of most types of wood, is not true of ebony. Therefore as an unqualified conclusion, the inductive reasoning that 'wooden things float' is

4   A useful text on this subject is *Thinking and Reasoning* by Garnham and Oakhill (1994).

wrong. For an inductive reasoning process to be reliable, it would be necessary to amass a lot of data along the lines of 'the ball is wood, and it floats', and then limit the conclusion to the experience offered by this data. This would have been done in the research into the Comet disaster, when the effects of different degrees of pressure on different sizes of cracks in the fuselage metal would have been measured, enabling the researchers to conclude that metal fatigue, which caused the cracks, was the root of the problem. However, in daily life the opportunities to conduct such controlled experiments are very rare, and in any case social researchers argue that conclusions from experiments with people's behaviours have to be very heavily qualified.

Many experiences are unusual or distinctive, if not quite unique, so the conclusions inferred from them have to be viewed with caution. Even when our experiences are built on a lot of comparable data, for example our travel to work times, leading, say, to the conclusion that travelling at the weekend takes only half the time, the unthinking reliance on this conclusion could lead us into trouble when, for example, roadworks, a marathon race along our route, or a heavy snowfall cause the time taken to be even greater than during weekdays.

Nevertheless, situations involving things and people can be repetitive and conclusions drawn from them. Early in my career I had the following experience, expressing it in the terms of logic noted above:

- 'A' came to a meeting directly from a pub, and it was a difficult meeting;

- 'B' came to a meeting directly from a pub, and it was a difficult meeting;

- 'C' came to a meeting directly from a pub, and it was a difficult meeting;

- Therefore, people coming to meetings from pubs lead to difficult meetings.

By and large, this seemed, and seems, a reasonable conclusion. People who have been drinking are usually less inhibited and more likely to express themselves forcefully, both of which can raise the tension if the subject of the meeting is contentious. However, again, the conclusion must be qualified, because not only are some meetings held in pubs and conducted in amicable and conciliatory tones, but – going back to my logic statement – I also noticed that when 'D' came to a meeting from a pub it was actually a *less* difficult meeting than normal, probably because he was more relaxed and less withdrawn than usual.

The principal conclusion on the use of logic in experiential learning in daily life is to seek to use it, because doing so requires one to observe and think about the experience, but to regard its outcomes with caution, being consciously aware of any surrounding circumstances which may have influenced them.

HOW WE MAKE SENSE 2: SYSTEMS THINKING

In Chapter 5 we met Tim who, when taking part as a member of a project team in his organization, came across systems thinking or systems theory.[5] He found it very useful when exploring a new part of the business because it helped him to see the whole entity, and how one part related to another. The essence of a system, rather than a collection of parts, is that when something happens in one area of the system, something else will be triggered in another area. Thus in a modern central heating system there is a thermostat which measures air temperature, and can be set at a given level, say 22°C; when the system is on, if the air temperature falls below 22°C the boiler will be activated and the radiators caused to emit heat until such time as the temperature reaches 22°C. When 22°C has been reached this information is fed back to the boiler, which then turns itself off. Old-fashioned central heating boilers and radiators, by contrast, were either on or off, regardless of the air temperature, and were not part of a system in this sense.

A useful definition[6] is:

> *A system is an entity that maintains its existence and functions as a whole through the interaction of its parts.*

So in the above example, the 'entity' is the central heating boiler, the radiators and the thermostat, and it 'functions as a whole' when the thermostat tells the boiler that the temperature has dropped – causing the boiler to heat more water and pump it through the radiators. An essential feature of systems of this kind is the existence of *feedback* mechanisms, so that something happening in one part of the system will be communicated to another, leading, possibly, to some sort of compensatory action.

---

5   *The Art of Systems Thinking* (1997) by Joseph O'Connor and Ian McDermott provides a helpful and accessible account of this subject.
6   O'Connor and McDermott (1997), page 2.

It is possible to view many parts of modern life as systems, such as the procedures in an office – which may seize up if a significant component, such as a photocopier, does not work; a rail network – which may grind to a halt in very bad weather; a manufacturing process, where the supplies of one item impinge directly on the production of another; a hospital – where the possible rate of admissions depends on the resources (doctors, nurses, admin procedures, beds, operating theatre capacity and so on) available. So if we are considering changing one element in a system, say the speed of the photocopier, the number of carriages in a railway, the procedure for admission to hospital, it would be essential to trace through the systems to see what impact such a change would have.

Systems thinking has developed in many disparate fields. Weather prediction and climatology, physics and cosmology, evolutional biology, medicine, management, logistics and economic planning are just some of the areas of modern living in which it makes a contribution.[7]

For Tim, learning about systems thinking from his involvement in the project, the experience was doubly valuable. He was able to use it to explore the system that was the subject of the project, and, even more helpful in the long run, he had learnt a way of thinking, a tool for exploring and understanding a wide variety of other organizations. Later in his career he was working at industry level, studying the impact of the actions of a number of different organizations, on each other, on suppliers, customers, regulators and even international administrators. The experience of working with a fairly simple system in his original project led to a large increase in Tim's ability to predict accurately the consequences of various types of change.

HOW WE MAKE SENSE 3: PATTERN RECOGNITION

Not many of the people who contributed to my research by talking about their experiences were as self-aware as Alan, a senior financial manager who worked on Wall Street, but he was able to say in general terms how he used the events of daily life to inform his future actions. In one part of his repertoire, he was

> *always looking for sequences of events, behaviours, phenomena in*
> *general, which have things in common. They may be good, or bad. I use*
> *a lens for this process which ranges from the detail to the middle and*
> *far distance.*

---

7   For an account of its growth and current usage see O'Connor and McDermott (1997), part 6.

Alan went on to say that for him this was now an established mental habit, a little like the 'muscle memory' which you acquire when you learn to ride a bike or ski, and it enabled him to scan a number of experiences, some apparently related and others apparently not, to see what trends they suggested, and what he should do about them.

Alan's words reminded me of a phrase which a leading industrialist had used when he was describing the kind of graduates his company was seeking to recruit and develop. He was wanting men and women who could 'spot trends, and take action'. In this balance between the reflective and the decisive, it is significant that the reflective phase comes first, and it is essentially this aspect that is the subject of this book.

How do we use spotted trends or recognized patterns? In principle, there appear to be two main uses. A trend which is plotting a steady but adverse change clearly requires some sort of intervention. Thus if we are looking at the cash flow of a small business, where the net incoming cash is steadily reducing month after month, alarm bells should start ringing. Or, if a colleague whose behaviour has hitherto been normal starts to be fractious, then awkward, then disruptive, then violent, again alarm bells would ring and the underlying causes be sought. These are examples of undesirable trends, but trends in the other direction, that of improvement, could also require attention, albeit less urgently. An increasing positive cash flow could open up the possibility of much needed capital investment, while an employee whose performance improves well beyond the norm could be a candidate for promotion. All the actions implied in the last four examples would be justified by reference to the trends which preceded them.

The trends described above have been progressive, but the second type of use of a trend is where there is already an established steady state, that is the trend shows constant values, but it is succeeded by a sudden change. Thus, if we are looking at a patient's blood pressure (see Chapter 10) and there is a sudden fall (or rise) from the normal, the cause should be sought and a remedy applied. This is an example of Festinger's cognitive dissonance reduction; cognitively, while we are intellectually satisfied with normal blood pressure, a sudden, sizeable reduction or increase would cause a dissonance – why has this happened? what underlies this change? how should we treat this patient? and so on. The mental pressure caused by this dissonance would lead us to find solutions to reduce the pressure of dissonance, and we would not be satisfied until the patient's blood pressure was restored to near normal. In this kind of case, the trend we have been observing initially established a normal, acceptable pattern, so that when something very abnormal happens, which we interpret as dangerous, action can be taken.

Most of the trends illustrated above are quantifiable and measurable, and as such easier to build up and spot. However, other, less quantifiable phenomena are also liable to change, and as such can often be seen as part of a pattern. Obvious examples include the 'cause and effect' consequences of behaviours that affect our personal health. The link between pollen and hay fever is well known, but less known is the link between red wine and stomach upsets: for a minority of people the toxins in red wine react in the stomach and cause vomiting, even after as little as half a glass. In extreme instances, the wine in, say, the sauce in a meat or vegetable casserole could be sufficient to provoke illness. In this type of case, the trend of 'red wine causes vomiting' may be difficult to spot, because it is only *red* wine which has the effect, and it does not need to be consumed from a glass. It would be a matter of considering all the variables around each attack of illness and trying to identify the recurrent one(s). (This is where a fellow participant's observations could be helpful in reminding one of the various foods consumed, and an informed non-participant could help in pointing to possible or likely causes – a doctor, of course, being a professional informed non-participant.)

These examples of pattern recognition are at the homespun end of the experiential spectrum, but at the other end the spotting of trends and their validation is, for example, epidemiology, an essential part of modern medicine. A good example of major studies in which cause and effect were recognized is in the relationship between smoking and lung cancer. Sir Austin Bradford Hill and others were able to show in 1950 that the likelihood of suffering from lung cancer increased proportionately with the number of cigarettes smoked per day. His work is described in lay terms by James Le Fanu,[8] who points out that at that time around 90 per cent of adults were smokers, so it required discriminating and sensitive statistical techniques to separate out the influence of smoking compared with all other causes of death. One of Bradford Hill's techniques was to start a longitudinal study in 1951 – a forward study over a longish period of time, as opposed to retrospective studies, which looked at past performance – amongst a cohort of 60,000 doctors, in which the death rates due to lung cancer for smokers was compared with that for non-smokers. Forty years later, it could be shown that 'those smoking twenty-five or more cigarettes a day have a twenty-five-fold increased risk of lung cancer compared to non-smokers'.[9]

---

8   In his 2000 book *The Rise and Fall of Modern Medicine*.
9   Le Fanu (2000), page 55.

Before leaving pattern recognition as a way of learning from experience, the point should be made that the process is far from instant, and indeed usually takes a significant time. Obviously, major studies like Bradford Hill's longitudinal survey take a great deal of time – many years, in that case – but less statistical phenomena may also require much time. Not only is there the time needed for the observations to be made, the reduction in cash flow or the worsening behaviour of the colleague in the examples mentioned earlier, but the underlying cause(s) may be obscure, and require significant thinking time to sort out the relevant from the less relevant, or irrelevant, causes. The place of *time* in the reflection and insight phase will be discussed in more detail in the section on eureka's below.

Finally, the same caveats on pattern recognition need to be entered as were for logical reasoning above. In fact, a trend is a series of statements of the kind we saw under inductive reasoning, and again an element of caution is required, especially when the trend is not yet entirely obvious. The surrounding circumstances need to be kept in mind.

HOW WE MAKE SENSE 4: CHANGING PERSPECTIVE

One of the processes which several of my research colleagues used to gain insights into their experiences was consciously to put themselves in the place, and as far as possible the minds, of other people. We have already seen how Jim felt compelled to change the way he prepared for meetings, anticipating the ways his words could be interpreted. Another colleague, Vince, learned a similar lesson from a different experience many years earlier. He had recently taken responsibility for the transport function of a manufacturing business when a strike in a related concern affected his drivers, who initially joined the strike for three days in sympathy. The issue Vince faced the following week was what to pay his drivers: the works agreements justified the deduction of three-fifths of the week's pay, but he took a different view. Putting himself in the place of his drivers he argued to himself that the loss of 60 per cent of a week's pay would be very serious, and as they were now working normally he thought it preferable to make up the pay to a normal week. He did so, and felt totally vindicated when the shop steward stopped on his way home, having received his pay, and said 'much appreciated'! This incident proved to be a turning point in his work in the business as industrial relations, and operating performance, improved significantly.

For both Jim and Vince, the importance of considering other people's points of view was an intellectual shift in their previous mindsets, brought about by their experiences. (Other people, with different personalities, might well naturally and automatically take this viewpoint, but for them there could be scope for learning different lessons, from other experiences.) This 'thinking as others think' is actually one facet of the larger process of *changing perspectives*, of seeking insights and enlightenment from looking at an experience, or an issue or belief, from different points of view.

In the more down to earth world of fruit picking, it is accepted that one can pick more apples, blackberries, plums or whatever, by changing positions. Having picked all that can be seen when standing in one position, bending down, or approaching the tree or shrub from a completely different angle, often reveals more fruit which had hitherto been invisible. This is the rationale for the devil's advocate, the person at the Papal Court whose duty and role is to propose objections to someone the Pope is considering for canonization. In order to obtain a balanced view of the potential saint, the advocate on the devil's side points to his or her demerits and failings. The extension of this practice in ordinary life is for someone to make the counter-arguments against a possible proposal, idea, or course of action. The advantage of this role is that it is generally seen as just that – a *role* which someone is playing for the sake of thoroughness.

As in the case of pattern recognition, significant help in seeking, and following up, different perspectives can often be given by the *informed non-participant*. He, she, or they, being detached from your experience, are probably more able to stand aside from your viewpoint, and help you to adopt a stance. They may well be able to play the devil's advocate role. However, as we observed earlier, to make this kind of contribution there must be a feeling of mutual respect between you and them, each party feeling able to say whatever seems appropriate, and to listen without prejudging.

A slight extension of seeking different perspectives to help in learning from experience is that of looking out of one's own box into nearby or related boxes. A good example of this is in the field of sport, where enterprising coaches in one sport will look at activities in others. The English Rugby Union defensive coach, Phil Larder, said:

> *Bright coaches have always looked at other sports. When I started [in rugby league] I spent three weeks with Bob Paisley's Liverpool [football], just looking and learning. The Wallabies [rugby union] took a lot from the Australian Rules game, and when American football caught on here, the best coaches travelled across the Atlantic to see how they did things. The idea of specialist defensive coaching in rugby union came*

> *from gridiron, where they had dedicated defensive teams. Those teams*
> *didn't sit around drinking coffee and watching the offensive players go*
> *through their drills; they worked at their skills, and worked bloody hard.*
> *That was the shaft of light for many of us.*[10]

Incidentally, this points up the significance of having a *learning orientation* with
an open-minded personality, as discussed in Chapter 7.

HOW WE MAKE SENSE 5: EUREKAS

These are moments of sudden insights, revelations, which present themselves
out of the blue. They have this Greek name as a result of the philosopher
Archimedes who, when he had been puzzling over a problem with the
king's crown, suddenly found the answer when he was in his bath; he leapt
out saying 'Eureka', meaning 'I have found it'. They are also called 'Ah-ha's',
'light bulbs' (because they suddenly illuminate), and occasionally 'epiphanies'.
Neuroscientists have been able to find out, by scanning the brains of people who
are solving paper and pencil problems, that one particular part of the brain, the
anterior superior temporal gyrus, just above the right ear, is particularly active
immediately before eurekas occur.[11]

They occur in almost every field and discipline. Consider the following:

- Henri Poincaré, mathematician, suddenly saw the key to some
  work he was doing into the theory and function of fuchsian groups
  as he was stepping on to a bus.[12]

- Freeman Dyson, physicist, after working intensively but without
  result at Princeton for six months, took a holiday in California;
  on his way back, on a Greyhound bus 'suddenly, in the middle of
  the night, when we were going through Kansas, the whole thing
  suddenly became clear ... it was a eureka experience for me'.[13]

- Harold Ridley, eye surgeon, had the notion of making intra-ocular
  lens implants when carrying out surgery for cataracts: it came 'with
  a flash of inspiration'.[14]

---

10 Chris Hewett (2004).
11 Jung-Beeman *et al.* (2004).
12 Hadamard (1949), page 13.
13 Csikszentmihalyi (1996), page 82.
14 Le Fanu (2000), page 82.

- JK Rowling, author, had the idea for Harry Potter when she was sitting on a stationary train between Manchester and London 'while gazing at cows … I can't tell you why or what really triggered it, but I saw the idea of Harry and the wizard school very plainly. I suddenly had this idea of a boy who didn't know who he was.'[15]

- Frank Sinatra, singer, early in his career, modelled his phrasing and breath control as a result of seeing and hearing Jascha Heifetz (world-famous violinist) at Carnegie Hall:[16] he observed that there was no perceptible break between the violin bow coming down and going up, and said 'It was my idea to make my voice work in the same way as a trombone or a violin.'

- Ken Aston, football referee, searching in 1966 for a way of communicating with football players with different languages, hit on the idea when driving down Kensington High Street, and having to stop at the traffic lights, of showing yellow and red cards.[17]

- Sir William Jones, diplomat and language scholar, was being posted to Calcutta and in 1788 was exploring the links between Sanskrit and Western languages, '[I] had a Eureka moment, and saw what was effectively a series of root connections between Sanskrit and other languages'.[18]

- Milton Glaser, designer, hired to help turn round New York and its citizens' self-image, coined the slogan 'I love NY'. Two days after agreeing it with the Mayor, he had 'a sudden flash of inspiration' while sitting in a taxi on the way to another meeting, and came up with 'I ♥ NY'.[19]

Eurekas should not be thought of as the exclusive province of exceptionally gifted individuals. They can occur when two old ideas meet – to form a new one. During my research I heard several examples of sudden insights coming out of the blue. Ken was presented with a problem about his house sale when he arrived at work one morning, and although he was unable to do anything about it during a heavy morning's meetings, when he went to the gym at lunchtime (as was his practice) a novel solution suddenly occurred to him. Bert

15 McGreevy (2004), page 36.
16 Summers and Swan (2005), page 66.
17 Chesterton (2005).
18 Bragg (2003), page 254.
19 Radio interview.

had quite a common experience when trying to solve crosswords, finding that after struggling with one for half an hour if he put it down and got on with his work, when he returned to it much later several answers to clues would immediately 'pop up'. Peter had a eureka during an exam: looking at all the questions at the start he decided to do two more straightforward answers first before returning to a more difficult one. When he did so, an angle on the question suddenly came to him, enabling him to give a much more comprehensive and imaginative answer than if he had attempted it at the beginning.

Some of these illustrations of eurekas are genuine cases of learning, in the sense that they uncovered natural laws which were there all along and were now revealed – Poincaré, Dyson and Jones – while others are examples of innovation, where their creators produced something which had not existed before – Rowling, Aston and Glaser. In all cases, although they arrive suddenly and unbidden, they are actually part of a larger process. The American psychologist Mihalyi Csikszentmihalyi (it's a Hungarian name, pronounced 'chick-shent-me-hi') worked with colleagues to study the thought processes of 91 highly creative men and women drawn from the complete spectrum of public life – arts, literature, painting/sculpture, music; science; engineering; business; politics – during the second half of the twentieth century, and summarized a sequence of events as follows:

The Role of Insight in the Creative Process*

Preparation: problem defined; work done by collecting data and viewing from different perspectives

Incubation: parallel processing in subconscious during periods away from specific problem

Insight: solution to problem envisioned, possibly with feelings of satisfaction or elation

Evaluation: solution attempted or applied. If inadequate, return to *preparation.*

* Adapted from Csikszentmihalyi and Sawyer (1995), page 338.

Figure 11.1 The role of insight in the creative process

The preparation phase generally entails a great deal of hard work. Sometimes, the problem being addressed is straightforward, but at other times 'the problem is the problem', when it is difficult to be clear about exactly what is the central issue. This phase often involves the amassing of many data, which in themselves may lead in contrary directions. For big, complex problems it may last for weeks or months. In each of the examples given above, even if no preparation phase is stated it can be assumed that the subject of the eureka was engaging its author for a long period before the insight came. Glaser, for example, would have been pondering his brief, and experimenting with different slogans, for energizing the people of New York to think positively about their city, which had been suffering a downturn of trade, increased violence and public corruption. Jones was learning the new (to him) language of Sanskrit and comparing it with Western languages, Sinatra was studying the craft of singing and the art of other performers, Aston was struggling with the problems of communication when two football teams and the referee all speak different languages and so on. All creative people would agree with the truism that their work is '99 per cent perspiration, 1 per cent inspiration'.

However long and arduous the phase of preparation, the next phase of *incubation* seems critical. This is not to say that problems are not solved *during* periods of hard work – clearly they are in some, perhaps many, circumstances, but for others, especially where a leap of imagination and true creativity is required, some time spent away from the workface seems necessary.

Csikszentmihalyi and Sawyer[20] offer an intriguing model of how the mind works in such situations. They suggest that the brain works at three levels of consciousness. At Level 1, *conscious attention* is given to selected issues, and this is done serially, one thing after another (even if the minds hops about), that is by the mind focusing on one matter at any particular moment. It may, of course, move from subject to subject very rapidly, but this is done in real time. At Level 2, *semiconscious filters* mediate what information is passed to and from the subconscious. At Level 3, *subconscious processing* occurs in a distributed, parallel manner, making it possible for multiple chunks of information to be viewed simultaneously. This enables connections to be made in a manner denied to the serially operating consciousness (Level 1); these connections may reveal insights which are then submitted, via the semiconscious filters to the conscious brain.

Incubation implies inactivity, or at least a shift of attention to some other subject. It is interesting that in several of the examples given above, movement – associated with transport, or driving – features in descriptions of eurekas,

---

20   Csikszentmihalyi and Sawyer (1995), pages 341–342.

and many people mention walking or jogging as conducive for new thinking. Gardening, housework and gym are also often mentioned. Turning to a new but very demanding subject does not generally seem to be productive – it is as though the mind needs to be on 'light duty' work for the Level 3 thinking to be productive. (An exception to this generalization could be Peter, who had the exam eureka mentioned above when he deferred a difficult question until after answering two easier ones. Even here, however, perhaps the fact that they were easier allowed his Level 3 thinking to proceed in parallel with the Level 1 question answering.)

An interesting issue arises concerning the place of *sleep* for providing incubation time. Robert Louis Stephenson is said to have been inspired to write *The Strange Case of Dr Jekyll and Mr Hyde* after sleeping, and Mendeleev, the Russian chemist, said that he formulated the critical rule for the periodic table of chemical elements after sleeping deeply (although in both cases there must have been substantial preparatory work beforehand). There is plenty of anecdotal evidence of people finding that, after a night's sleep, a problem which was obscure and intractable the day before becomes much clearer and soluble. I had a colleague who used to say 'don't decide today what you can decide tomorrow!' This might sound like a recipe for procrastination, but in fact he was a very decisive person, perfectly capable of taking hard decisions when the need arose. He had found that, if it was possible, time, or incubation, gave his brain the opportunity to clarify, find new solutions and sort things out, so that a deferred decision was likely to be a better one.

So sleep appears to be a special form of incubation, a period when connections between parallel thoughts in the subconscious can be bridged, but it is not a selective process, concentrating on the positive and filtering out unpleasant, negative connections. The historical writer Antony Beevor, for example, who has written about some of mankind's most desperate situations, such as the starvation which occurred during the siege of Stalingrad, said that during the actual moments of research, when reading documents describing the most dire of human conditions, his mind remained focused on the texts and their implications for his writing: the horror of what he was reading would only hit him 24 or 36 hours later, often at night.[21]

After the *insight* phase there may be a cluster of activities summed up in the *evaluation* phase, depending on the nature of the problem or issue in question. Sometimes the eureka provides a clear and comprehensive answer which enables implementation to be made very quickly, but at other times the insight

---

21   An interview in the *Independent* (2005).

needs clarification, development and other work. Quite often it might lead back to more preparation work, and the cycle could begin again, although a second eureka would be less likely to be as vivid as the first.

Before leaving eurekas, it is worth pointing out that they are not necessarily positive, opening up new ideas, ways of thinking and acting. Some can be negative, sounding warnings that an idea, trend or other phenomenon will lead to problems or worse. When I was discussing this aspect with one of my research colleagues he referred to it as 'a little niggle' that he had learned to pay attention to. If he felt uneasy about something, he found it was worth going back and reviewing it to isolate what exactly caused his unease. (This further points up the importance of *emotions* as an important element in learning from experience.) I could relate to his comments, having once woken up in the morning realizing that a project I was contemplating was severely misplaced! Although less exciting than their creative cousins, negative eurekas are clearly almost as valuable in saving us from grief and/or futile activity.

HOW WE MAKE SENSE 6: RULES OF THUMB – HEURISTICS

'Heuristics' are defined as 'principles used in making decisions when all possibilities cannot be fully explored'. Derived from the Greek word 'to find', heuristic methods feature in education when pupils are encouraged to explore their subject matter for themselves, finding out its essential characteristics, and cognitive psychologists develop them to explain how people solve certain types of problems. Interestingly, heuristics are used extensively in artificial intelligence (AI).[22] AI machines are usually programmed to ignore and discard a wide range of possible actions which, although theoretically valid, have been recognized by the designers as so unlikely as to be discountable. The programmers recognize that machines, like people themselves, work better when focusing on the realistic rather than the whole range of the theoretic.

Heuristics are often described, as in the above sub-heading, as rules of thumb, but this seems slightly inaccurate. The term 'rule of thumb' is derived from the practice of using one's thumb, of known width – usually about 1" – as the basis for measuring the height of a distant object. (It is an elaboration of Baden Powell's technique, in *Scouting for Boys,* which describes how, if you know how far you are from, say, a tree, and that your thumb is 1" wide, you can calculate the approximate height of the tree.) However, I will follow common practice.

---

22 An interesting exposition of human creativity and AI is given in *The Creative Mind* by Margaret Boden (2004).

How do they figure in learning from experience? They have significance in two respects; first, they can often be helpful in the final stages of validating the lessons than one derives from the experience, and we will look at this aspect more fully in the next chapter on *credibility checking*. Second, as we reflect on the lessons offered by experience, heuristics or rules of thumb are often the only possible satisfactory outcomes. Real life, unlike scientific experiments, rarely allows repetition in controlled conditions, so the conclusions we draw from an experience are inevitably tentative to some degree.

As we ponder on a recent experience we naturally tend to compare it with earlier experiences, if possible of a similar nature, and we tend to draw out the lessons, the generalities from the whole which can be applied in the future. They enable us to make predictions with more confidence than if we reflect on only one. In any case, Festinger's work on cognitive dissonance, discussed earlier in this section, showed that most people are content when the dissonance has been *reduced,* not necessarily eliminated. We are content to live with rules of thumb rather than spend time and energy trying to develop the heuristic into a general rule capable of rigorous validation.

Let us look in a little detail at an heuristic which I deduced during one phase of my life, and which served me well. I was responsible in my organization for overseeing the selection and recruitment of senior professionals during a time when, due to expansion, quite a number were needed. Starting from an experience base of nil, because during the previous years we had been slimming down and had recruited no one, I soon worked out that between starting the ball rolling and having the new 'recruit' at his or her desk, would take between four and six months. So this was my rule of thumb, which was used to advise my senior colleagues who were contemplating recruitment. It could be very wrong, as when exactly the right kind of person, known to the colleague, was currently out of work and could join in a week, or where a combination of a difficult labour market and chosen candidates giving back-word (the withdrawal of a promise) resulted in a delay of nearly 12 months before someone suitable arrived. However, as a general rule, the times taken to decide the detail of job, the person specification, advertise, select a long list, interview, decide, agree salary and conditions, followed by the notice the chosen candidate had to give the present employer, all added up to four months if we were fortunate, and six months for a more typical scenario.

One of my research colleagues, Al, discovered an heuristic which served him well when he was tackling what was probably the biggest challenge of his career. He was a civil engineer, responsible for laying a number of large water mains at a time when, due to an apparently never-ending drought, the need to access further water supplies was paramount. The established practice for laying water mains was to start at one end and proceed to the other, typically at a rate of around 1 km per month, but this was totally unacceptable in the present circumstances. All the work was contracted out to subcontractors, Al's role being that of selecting the contractors and then facilitating and overseeing their progress. In one job, Firm X had laid a main over 7 km in three weeks, entirely satisfactorily. Now Al needed to construct an important 55 km main, and, in what he described as a minor eureka, he realized that if the total project were divided into five subprojects, each tackled by its own subcontractor working simultaneously with the others, the overall construction time could be reduced from the traditional 55 months to six to ten weeks. His rule of thumb of 7 km in three weeks, together with the mould-breaking concept of simultaneous starts, enabled a major job to be accomplished in an acceptable time.

Of course, the use of a rule of thumb like 7 km in three weeks was risky on several fronts. Mains-laying is very dependent on the nature of the ground in which the pipes are laid; not all contractors are equally efficient; the interfaces between different contractors could bring unanticipated problems; problems of access to remote sections of the route could slow down the whole; and so on. Moreover, the 7 km in three weeks could have been achieved only in the most favourable conceivable conditions. These were some of the predictable areas of concern which Al and his team recognized, and it was their role to work with contractors and enable them to work as expeditiously as possible. The heuristic on which the overall project was based, used with caution, proved to be pivotal in a very notable achievement.

Many, but not all, heuristics are expressed in quantifiable terms. The above two examples of four to six months for recruitment, and 7 km in three weeks are typical. Other examples which readily come to mind are £40 per square foot for converting a barn (actually this is a mid-point figure, between £20 for a very simple job using inexpensive fittings and £60 for a complex job using highest quality fittings); three hours overall to cook a three-course dinner; 60 miles per hour for long-distance motorway driving. Again, the caveats are crucial. Three hours for dinner assumes, for example, no overnight marinating, or fiddly starters or sweets on the one hand, but also that the dinner does not consist of tinned soup and an omelette on the other.

Non-quantifiable heuristics are also common, but probably less overtly quoted because their bases are not so open to discussion and scrutiny, and in recent years because they fall foul of political correctness in the fields of racism, sexism, ageism and the rest. I had a colleague whose rule of thumb was to distrust men who wore suede shoes. An example of an heuristic that is sometimes given in the literature is 'When climbing an unknown mountain in fog, without a map, take upward steps'! It seems obvious, but illustrates the provisional nature of such advice, because straight upward steps may take you to a shoulder or false summit, whereas diagonal upward steps could take you to the true summit. Checklists often emerge as heuristics because based on one experience, say going on holiday to a hot climate, we use its lessons to prepare for another similar holiday. Proverbs may also act as rules of thumb: least said, soonest mended; a stitch in time saves nine; coming events cast their shadows before them – encapsulate lessons which experiences over the years have taught me. And a proverb of my own making: 'a tired brain makes clumsy hands'.

Heuristics or rules of thumb may be founded on shaky ground, open to challenge, and sometimes downright quirky, but they nevertheless contribute to the products of reflection and insight, as we shall see in the next section.

PRODUCTS

The possible outcomes of reflection and insight are so many and varied as almost to defy any sort of systematic treatment. When we recall the range of experiences that people can enjoy or endure, the personal qualities that each person brings to them through their individual *learning orientations*, and the extent and range of the inputs from *own observations* and experience to *formal knowledge*, it seems foolhardy even to attempt an assessment in a few pages. Nevertheless, the following classification is offered in the hope that it will help to point up some of the processes discussed in the preceding section, and to show how experience plays a part in our relations with the past, the present, and the future. While there is inevitably some overlap, the structure of outcomes which seems most helpful is:

- knowledge

- understanding

- judgement, and

- skills.

By *knowledge* I mean mainly facts. Much knowledge is contained in books and other written media, such as facts about the physical and animate world, its history, artefacts, political and belief systems, and very often experiential learning builds on this knowledge. For example, before visiting Paris for the first time I can look at a map of the city and its Metro system, seeing how different lines serve different localities, but only when I have been there and used the Metro do I recognize the station signs (which are in a completely different format from their equivalents in, say, London or New York), know how long it can take to change lines at the *co-respondences*, experience the walking musicians who travel up and down the trains, and so on. Knowledge often constitutes answer to the questions what?, where?, when? and who?

During my research, this type of information was relatively infrequently offered as examples of learning from experience. When it was mentioned it was often placed in the context of learning when taking up a new job. Thus Dan, mentioned earlier in Chapter 9, had a steep learning curve when he became a general manager and had to work with disciplines which were new to him. Anne valued her mentor because of his willingness to give her articles and extracts which built up her knowledge base of her new role and business. Keith spoke of the value of his MBA in helping him with the language of different functions with whom he subsequently worked quite closely.

Understanding usually builds on knowledge, being founded on answers to questions why? and how? So we might have knowledge of an organisation, what it does, who works in it, where it is located, and so on, but our understanding of the organization tells us how it operates, what are the relationships between different parts of it, how it fits into the larger scheme of things and so on. In one sense, this too is knowledge in so far as it could be acquired from books or brochures, but real, in-depth understanding probably only comes from personal involvement with it, from experiencing its systems and workings from inside or closely from outside – perhaps as a customer or supplier. Understanding of oneself, one's motivations, likes and dislikes, is also based almost entirely on the experiences we have had. It is only possible to say whether I like a certain food, for example, when I have actually tasted it, although it would be possible to make a guess at my reaction by reference to other foods I have experienced and like or dislike.

Examples of experiential learning contributing to understanding were perhaps the most common, and quite often in circumstances where the knowledge base was relatively unchanged. Earlier in this chapter, in the section on processes, I described how Tim learned of the value of systems thinking.

He already had a conceptual knowledge of the different parts of the systems, but his work in the project team enabled him to see and understand how the different parts interacted. Rick, being eased out of his finance job in London, came to understand the motivations of the new boss, and realized that it was up to him, and him alone, to look after his future. It dawned on Jim, during his difficult meeting, that he had failed to anticipate how his arguments would be received, an understanding which altered the way he prepared for all his meetings in the future.

Judgement in turn builds on knowledge and understanding. Judgemental statements, such as 'We are not in a financial crisis', 'Watch him, he's a crook!', and 'That was an excellent presentation', assume both a knowledge of the basic facts, relating to a financial situation, a man's behaviour and the content and delivery of the presentation respectively, and an understanding of the dynamics of each situation. They enable the authors of the statements to use their critical acumen to reassure, warn and congratulate, and in so doing they draw on that part of the author's personality (in their *learning orientation*) relating to objectivity and assessment. They enable the authors to compare and contrast the realities, which are the subjects of comment, with other possibilities, experienced or imagined, and to conclude the statements made above.

For many of my research colleagues, understanding and judgement were wrapped closely together, the one leading quickly and inevitably to the other. Thus Jeannie understood her sense of unease at being unable to talk to her bereaved friend, and – given Jeannie's personality – led to her concluding that she could not live with this deficiency in her repertoire of responses. Similarly Jim, understanding his inability to make his arguments acceptable to his colleagues, could not tolerate his incapacity, and took steps to make it good.

From understanding and judgement come our determination to develop new *skills*. I understand from travelling and meeting people in other countries the value of being skilled in their languages. (This is more than simple knowledge, being based on the emotional charges of the pleasures obtained from full and empathetic communication, and the miseries of failures to communicate.) My experience of attempting to learn languages leads me to form a judgement to persevere with French, because I can see a fairly extensive use for it in the future, while not attempting to learn, say, Hindi before visiting India; I recognize that I find learning languages fairly difficult, and decide that the benefits accruing from being conversant with Hindi are not worth the efforts needed.

Not many of my research colleagues described the development of skills arising from their learning from experience, but for most it was implicit. We tend to think of 'skills' as being bodily functions, especially manual skills such as being good with the use of tools, sports equipment such as tennis racquets or cricket bats, or musical instruments, but for many people their greatest skills are cognitive, such as thinking in abstract or practical modes, and communicating outwards, orally or in writing, and inwards, through listening or observing. Thus Jim's description of his learning, from the awful meeting with his union colleagues, concluded when he described his understanding of his own past deficiencies and hence his future needs, but my own observation of him in his subsequent career is that he built on that understanding by becoming, over time, very skilful in being able to anticipate his audience's needs and hence to address them.

During a particularly interesting interview discussion, Mike described how he had learned from several early bosses certain characteristics which had served him well throughout his career, namely confidence, meticulousness and resilience. These are personality traits, but not ones which he felt he had had to any marked extent, yet he thought that he had become reasonably adept – I would have said skilled – at conveying them in his work. As a close working colleague over several years I would confirm his belief. Mike had become skilled at conveying to other people his persona which included those characteristics, which very probably had the effect of strengthening whatever inborn propensities he had in these areas.

PARADOXES, SUPERSTITIONS AND ERRORS

In the whole of this chapter so far we have been assuming that whatever experiences we have had would, in fact, yield lessons which contributed to our learning. This is a reasonable assumption, because usually when we put even a little effort into reflecting on an experience we can make at least some sense of it, and use it in the future. Yet this is not invariably the case, and it would be disingenuous to imply that it was.

Some experiences defy comprehension, at least immediately afterwards. This could be attributable to almost any of the elements discussed above, but most often it is probably because of either problems with data – too little, or too confusing, or with our *learning orientation* – a personality trait getting in the way, or we are possessed of the wrong kind of ability.

So then what? It probably depends on the experience. If its impact on us was relatively small, we would almost certainly forget it, and it would be parked in our subconscious along with a thousand and one other small events which illustrate life's curiosities. If, however, it was a powerful experience, one which refuses to go away, we would probably embrace it as a paradox, incorporate it as a superstition, or invest it with a meaning which was simply wrong.

A paradox exists when we encounter something which contradicts all our previous knowledge and belief. Examples could be 'Jill has unfailing good manners: Jill has just been unbelievably rude'; 'the ship is unsinkable: the ship has just sunk'; 'my employer always looks after me: my employer has just made me redundant'; and 'on a clear day, the sun shines brightly at midday: today, when it is clear, the sun has just disappeared'. Because, as Festinger pointed out, we are uncomfortable with this state of mental affairs, we seek answers, but sometimes no credible answer can be found.

How we proceed then probably depends on our learning orientation including memory. The combination of personality and ability, mediated by our recall of similar circumstances, is likely to influence us, initially, in deciding whether to pursue our attempts to resolve the paradox. Some people have a high degree of what psychologists call 'ambiguity tolerance', in other words they can live quite comfortably in the knowledge that there are paradoxes and other things, perhaps many things, they do not understand or know. There is the saying that an effective person is someone who can hold two opposing thoughts in their head, and still take action, and this is someone who would have a high degree of ambiguity tolerance. Towards the other end of the scale is someone who has a low threshold of ambiguity tolerance, who needs to come to some sort of resolution before moving on.

Perhaps the most important aspects of *learning orientation* are those personality traits concerned with self-belief and self-confidence, but ability, the combination of intelligences and their development, also play a part. Thus someone with a high degree of self-worth, who is content to live with a paradox in a familiar field, at least for the time being, may nevertheless seek a solution in another intelligence field in which they are much less able, that is have less development. This could account for the fact that someone who is very eminent in one field may hold irrational beliefs in another.

Superstitions are often the responses to paradoxes. We have seen the solar eclipse example of an apparent paradox given above, and noted earlier that primitive man, searching for a reason for such an anomalous and frightening event, attributed the cause to the gods, believing that they were being punished for earlier misdeeds. Indeed, in the minds of primitive man, not to mention those of his more sophisticated descendants, the gods provided a useful explanation for a wide range of paradoxes relating to climate, fertility and all chance events. The 'will of the gods' provides a ready explanation for situations where cognitive dissonance needs to be reduced. Sometimes the will of a more powerful god needs to be invoked, such as when we qualify a prediction by saying 'touch wood' – where 'wood' = the Cross.

Superstitions are arguably a special class of explanations for experiences which are just plain wrong. In the grass seed example in Chapter 3, the first explanation for the failure of seed to germinate was that the site was too shaded. This was a plausible reason, because shade is indeed an important factor for some plant viability, and had I not had the subsequent experience of sowing new seed with complete success I might have concluded that lack of light was *the* important cause of failure.

Most people would admit, at least privately, that they have misinterpreted experiences and drawn conclusions, and possibly acted on them, which later proved to be wrong. Misjudging people is a common experiential error; we may believe someone is trustworthy, on the basis of some sort of experience, only to learn later that they are quite the opposite. Or we may mark somebody as disagreeable only to find in them, later on, the most attractive qualities. After seeing it used extensively by friends we may buy some artefact or garment with great hopes for ourselves, only to find it is totally unsuitable and a waste of money. We may invest time and money in a project, believing that it will yield great returns, only to discover that its advocates had lied about it and the whole thing was a sham. And so on, sadly.

Why do we make these errors? Again, the answers may lie in any of the elements in any combination in the Model. We may have insufficient evidence, that is too few *observations*, by ourselves or others, or we may have failed to research sufficiently in *formal knowledge*. We may be too trusting, or too critical, or have just forgotten earlier experience – namely suffering from a lapse of *memory*. Or we may have been insufficiently rigorous in our *reflection*, and as a result have had insights which did not fit the facts as we know them.

The good news in all of this is that there is a final stage in the learning process which is designed to scrutinize the lessons learnt and the conclusions drawn from an experience, to test that, as far as we can be sure, they are valid and reliable. In the Model this is the element *'credibility checking'* – the subject of the next chapter.

POINTS FOR EXPLORATION

It is a good idea to consolidate your thinking on the contents of this chapter by using it to *explore and illustrate a recent experience*. In this case, it makes sense to go through in reverse order, namely: a) Products, b) Processes, and c) Prompts.

PRODUCTS

- What did the experience contribute to your knowledge, understanding, judgement or skills? If it built up judgement or skills, how have you used them since? If there has been no use so far, how could you envisage using them?

PROCESSES

Which of the following ways of making sense did you use in this experience:

- explanations through reasoning

- systems thinking

- pattern recognition

- changing perspective

- eurekas

- rules of thumb – heuristics

- others (summarize the main features)?

- how would you illustrate its/their use in this experience?

PROMPTS

- What event(s) got you started?

- Did it/they change during the experience, and if so, how?

CHAPTER 12

Credibility Checking Our Experience Bank

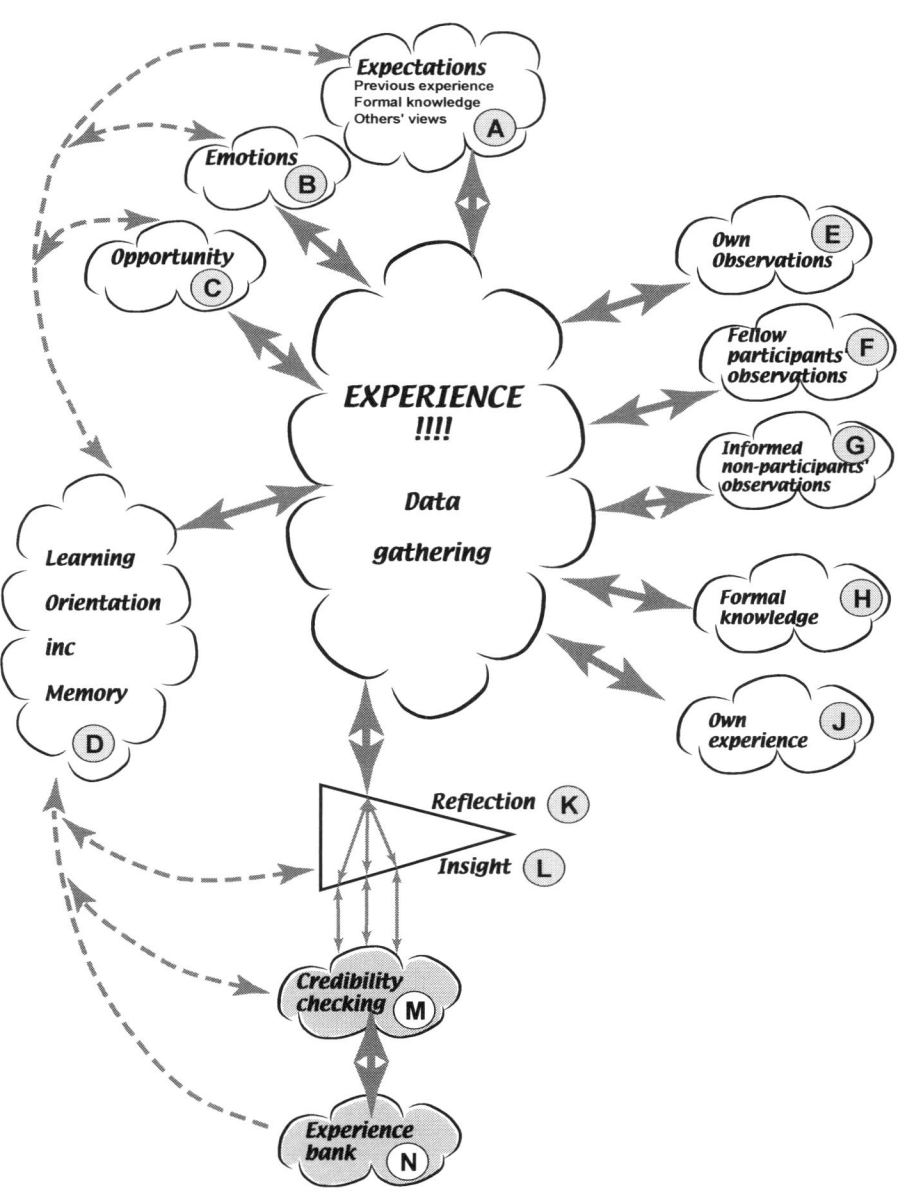

INTRODUCTION

During the development of the Model, the significance of *credibility checking* emerged very early on, as soon, in fact, as I had interviewed my first research colleagues. One of them, Alan, the finance specialist working on Wall Street, emphasized the importance of 'critiquing', telling oneself the truth. 'Kick your own tires! Close the office door so no-one hears or sees you, and say it like it is.' His phrase 'kick your own tires', a very American, car-based society phrase, stayed with me from then on. He meant, of course, make sure that you are proceeding safely, that what you are learning makes sense, and that what you are planning will work – and be totally objective, facing up to possible errors, nonsense, or wishful thinking.

Very few other colleagues were as explicit, but all would testify to the importance of ensuring that what they had learned was true, or if validation was impossible, of recognizing that a lesson was provisional, and treating it with caution.

The term '*credibility checking*' in this final element of learning from experience is self-explanatory. If we have an experience, particularly if it is one-off and distinctly different from anything we have known before, gather data about it, reflect on it and derive some insights from it, we would want to be as sure as reasonably possible that the conclusions make sense, and could form the basis for future action. Jim, for example, in Chapter 2, concluded that the problem in his difficult meeting with his union colleagues lay with his own inability to see the issue under discussion from their points of view. Other possible conclusions, such as that they were simply stupid, or that he had not expressed himself sufficiently clearly, did not accord with his observations; he knew they were not stupid, because he had worked extensively with them in the past, and he had obviously been clear because they answered his every point. Credibility checking means taking steps to ensure that the conclusions or lessons drawn from an experience are justified in terms of the various data available.

The neuroscientist and Reith Lecturer V. S. Ramachandran[1] has put forward an interesting hypothesis on our ability to be self-critical, based on his work with patients who have suffered major brain damage as a result of accidents or strokes. He describes a condition known as *anosognosia*, a patient's inability to perceive that one side of one's body is paralysed, and who lives in a state of denial in this respect. In one case, for example, a woman whose left side was completely

---

1   Dr Ramachandran describes his work in *Phantoms in the Brain*, Ramachandran and Blakeslee (1998).

paralysed as a result of a stroke which impaired the right hemisphere of her brain, insisted that she had tied her shoelaces, a task that required both hands. It has long been recognized that the two hemispheres have different functions, and Dr Ramachandran's theory is that one of the left brain's roles is:

> to create a belief system or model and fold new experiences into that belief system … The right hemisphere's strategy, on the other hand, is … to question the status quo and look for global inconsistencies. When the anomalous information reaches a certain threshold, the right hemisphere decides that it is time to force a complete revision of the entire model and start from scratch.[2]

In the cases of patients whose right hemisphere has been damaged, their ability to assess their new condition may be radically impaired, and they insist that they are able to function as before, for example in tying shoelaces.

It is interesting to suppose, therefore, that in normal people, whose brains are not damaged, the credibility checking process represents a balance between the two hemispheres, the left coming up with theories, perhaps using methods described in the previous chapter, which fit in with, and tend to re-enforce, pre-existing beliefs, whilst the right has a watching brief and challenges emerging lessons when they fail in some way. People who are naturally very sceptical, seeing the problems and limitations of the conclusions from their experiences, could therefore have relatively more assertive right hemispheres, while those who are trusting and rarely self-critical use their right hemispheres to a much lesser extent.

Just as 'learned behaviours' contribute to our *learning orientations* (Chapter 7), so some types of credibility checking can be institutionalized and become automatic as we can see in 'The discovery of cortisone' below.

THE DISCOVERY OF CORTISONE

In James Le Fanu's book *The Rise and Fall of Modern Medicine*, in which he describes some of the most significant developments in medicine, before going on to discuss some of its principal stresses and problems, a chapter is devoted to the discovery of cortisone, the amazing group of steroid chemicals used to

---

2   Ramachandran and Blakeslee (1998), page 136. This is the central point of the section from pages 131–137.

treat upwards of 90 diseases.[3] Over a period of 20 years Dr Philip Hench, a physician at the Mayo Clinic in Rochester, Minnesota, sought and eventually found a treatment for rheumatoid arthritis (RA), for which he was awarded the Nobel Prize in 1950, and the story of his work illustrates very well the place of credibility checking as he learned from his work.

The Discovery of Cortisone

In 1928 Dr Hench was treating an RA patient for jaundice when the patient mentioned that the RA pain and swelling in his joints went away at the onset of the jaundice, and remained free for seven months after it had cleared up. Hench believed that the two were related, and over the next few years he came across similar cases. Jaundice is a condition caused by liver problems, and Hench gave his RA patients bile salts, diluted bile, liver extracts, and transfused them with blood from jaundice patients – all with negative results.

Later he observed that RA patients who were pregnant also had remission of their RA condition. Moreover, not only was RA alleviated, but other ailments such as hay fever, asthma and the neurological disorders myasthenia gravis also improved. Pregnancy is a natural condition, so Hench argued that the body naturally produces something, Substance X, which has the beneficial effects on RA and other ills.

He approached Professor Edward Kendall, also at the Mayo Clinic, who was working on the isolation of the chemicals produced in the adrenal glands, coming up with several substances he labelled Compounds A, B, E, and F. Hench and Kendall speculated that one or more of these compounds could be 'Substance X', but the production of the pure compounds was uneconomic and could not be tested until after the Second World War, although Hench recorded this as an exciting possibility in his notebook.

By 1948, the drug company Merck was able to produce a little of Compound E, later called cortisone, and Hench administered it to a patient with severe RA. The effects were almost immediately dramatic; within a day she was able to move more comfortably, and within a week to go shopping for several hours. Over the next few months 13 more patients were treated with similar results. In doing this, Hench and

---

3   Chapter 2, on the discovery of cortisone, concludes with an extract from Martindale's *The Extra Pharmacopeia* which lists the diseases responsive to steroid therapy, page 25.

the patients were lucky that Hench had chosen the right dosage (very large by later standards), and had used crystals of an appropriate size which permitted the correct rate of solution. Changes in either of these variables would have produced less effective results.

However, there was an irony in Hench and Kendall's discovery. When used with RA patients the side effects were quite serious, and cortisone has only a limited value. Nevertheless, for an amazingly wide range of other ailments it is invaluable in helping the body to live through a 'crisis', allowing other remedies – natural or artificial – to effect a cure.

The first set of credibility checks came when Dr Hench's experiments with liver products failed to replicate the remission which jaundice appeared to confer. In these cases, and throughout the account, the test which credibility checking applies is whether the patient enjoys some alleviation of their joint pains and swellings, and it would have been very clear that the results were negative. However, the presented evidence of several patients' improvements in RA when suffering from jaundice took Hench's thinking beyond the conventional belief at the time, namely that RA was caused by some sort of infection.

The next major step forward was the realization, provided by RA patients whose symptoms were cleared when they were pregnant, and that other illnesses were also reduced, that the body was providing its own relief through the production of 'Substance X', which was naturally produced during pregnancy. Le Fanu does not mention the testing of any other possible secretions until Hench's work with Kendall brought into consideration the compounds produced in the adrenal gland, so presumably there was none. However, when compound E, later called cortisone, was checked in severe RA cases the results were 'positive/negative'. Cortisone's credibility was positive in so far as it yielded very beneficial effects on the joint pains and swellings, but negative in terms of the unwanted side-effects, such as moon face, perforated ulcers and the bruising of vertebrae.

The results of these credibility checks seem unequivocal in the sense that the initial interventions they tested, the liver products, were negative, while those using cortisone were positive, albeit with negative side-effects. It is worth observing here that the sequence Hench was following, and that followed by countless medical and scientific researchers, resembles very closely that described by Kolb and discussed in Chapter 2. Figure 2.1 (page 12) showed the cyclical sequence of concrete experience; reflective observation; abstract conceptualization and active experimentation.

So initially Hench observed the effects of jaundice on RA (concrete experience); he wondered if the two could be connected (reflective observation); he thought that the liver may have some beneficial effect on RA (abstraction conceptualization); and he tried the effects of bile salts, liver extracts, and so on on RA patients (active experimentation); but he found that they had no effect (concrete experience). In this sequence the credibility check is the active experimentation leading to the second concrete experience. However, a later concrete experience was his observation that the pregnant RA patient had remission of her symptoms, and the sequence started again.

In general terms, therefore, the active experiments that lead to a subsequent concrete experience act as the credibility checks. They either prove, or disprove, the outcomes of abstract conceptualizations. If one proves it, the way is open for the same experiment to be repeated – by the same researcher, but also by other people, in different places and different times – but if the experiment disproves it the researcher can reflect further on why this was so, and possibly come up with a second theory (abstract conceptualization) to test with further experiments. This is the sequence which the researchers looking into the Comet aircraft disaster (Chapter 10) would have followed to lead to the conclusion that metal fatigue caused the planes to crash.

The problem with this sequence or model of experiential learning, as we saw in Chapter 2, is that in normal life, life outside the laboratory or hospital, the opportunities to repeat experiences, making small adjustments to see the consequences are rare. Hench could experiment with different liver-related substances, varying the dosage and its administration, gradually eliminating the various possibilities, whereas Jim, following his difficult union meeting, probably had one further chance to redeem the situation before there was a total breakdown of confidence between him and his men.

Before leaving Dr Hench and the discovery of cortisone, it is worth illustrating some of the other features of the learning Model put forward in this book. Initially, Hench's *expectations* were not confirmed when his patient drew his attention to the effects of jaundice – at that time he thought RA was caused by an infection. His curiosity (*emotion*) was roused by this apparent linkage, and he took the *opportunities* of other patients' experience of jaundice to confirm the initial observation. Hench's personality (*learning orientation*) seems to have made him a formidable researcher; Le Fanu describes him as having 'relentless determination' and the strength of character to overcome a severely cleft palate with a loud voice. His ability was considerable, being a well-established physician in a prestigious clinic. In addition to his *own observations,* he obviously made use of *participant's observations,* for the starting point for his quest was the doctor patient's comment, he worked closely with Professor Kendall during the later stages of the research, and he contributed to, and drew from, *formal knowledge* during the course of his work (Le Fanu cites technical papers written during the 1930s and 1940s). He was clearly *reflecting* on the outcomes of his interventions, gaining the *Insight* that remission of RA symptoms could come about through natural processes, viz. pregnancy. His *credibility checking* was described above.

OTHER FORMS OF CREDIBILITY CHECKING

The systematic testing of conclusions adopted by scientists and researchers in near-laboratory conditions is not normally available in more ordinary situations, yet the credibility checking of the outcomes of experiences is nevertheless often necessary and always advisable. The question of whether something is 'true' raises practical and philosophical questions,[4] but here we are concerned with the reliance that can be placed on a conclusion or insight that has emerged from reflection.

Professor Tony Watson[5] has identified three ways of deciding the 'truth' of something which could not be verified by systematic experimentation. These are *correspondence* theories, *coherence/plausibility* theories, and *pragmatist* theories.

Correspondence theories of truth are used to decide on the accuracy of a report of what actually happened. Thus a jury is asked to conclude whether the account put forward by the prosecution is, beyond reasonable doubt, a truthful picture of what an accused person is said to have done. It may decide on quite disparate sources like motive, scientific evidence, evidence of opportunity, eyewitness testimony and so on. The prosecution will seek to build up a picture of actions by the accused which 'correspond' most closely to what it asserts was the truth. Equally, of course, the defence challenges all this detail.

---

4   For example, the entry under 'truth' in the *Oxford Companion to Philosophy* lists six different, and to some extent competing, theories of truth.
5   Tony Watson is Professor of Organizational Behaviour, and has written *Organising and Managing Work: Organisation, Managerial and Strategic Behaviour in Theory and Practice* (2001). The three theories are included in the *Oxford Companion* mentioned above.

Coherence/plausibility theories of truth address the likelihood of something having happened, using background information as the test. Thus if someone we know is alleged to have done or said something, to have stolen or lied, we might judge the 'truth' of the allegation by the extent to which it fits in with what we know about the person. The problem with this test of truth is, of course, that people can act out of character, and do things one would not expect of them. A normally truthful person might have lied in particular circumstances. This is the reason why juries in a criminal trial, for example, are never told an accused person's criminal record lest it influence them in reaching a verdict for or against: just because someone has stolen in the past does not mean to say that he or she has stolen in this particular case.

Both these theories, while rooted in the present, tend to look backwards, at how, for example, a statement corresponds with the facts as we know them, or how it coheres with what we already believe to be the case.

Pragmatist theories, on the other hand, tend to look forward: John Dewey, the American philosopher and educationalist, said that 'Knowledge ... is an instrument or organ of successful action.'[6] The pragmatic theory of truth, to quote the *Oxford Companion to Philosophy* (pages 709–711):

> *is to be understood in terms of practice. The notion of truth as a relation of correspondence between belief and reality is not rejected but clarified by reference to actions, future experiences, etc. ... Dewey identifies truth ('warranted assertibility') with the solution of a problem. Inquiry, he holds, starts from a 'problematic situation' and, if successful, ends with a situation that is so 'determinate' and 'unified' that hesitancy to act has been eliminated.*

Tony Watson illustrates the pragmatist theory by comparing the choice we might need to make between believing the promotional literature of a tourist resort with that of an independent guidebook. Another example would be comparing the advertisement for a product, say a washing machine, with an article in *Which?* magazine comparing several different makes of washing machine. We would be likely to ask ourselves in each case which is the 'truer'? – probably concluding in each case that the independent version was the more likely. The ultimate test, however, would be, to use Dewey's term, the 'successful action', that is which information about the tourist destination is the more

---

6   An extensive account of the pragmatist philosophers' lives, times and works is given in *The Metaphysical Club* by Louis Menand (2002). The quotation from Dewey is on page 361.

comprehensive, or which prediction of the washing machine's performance is the more accurate.

In real life, credibility checks may include elements of all three theories. Following his awful meeting, Jim may well have tested his insight, that he had failed to consider the way his arguments would be received, by reflecting that (i) he and his union colleagues had indeed been arguing from different premises (correspondence theory), (ii) his own performance was indeed centred on *his* arguments, having done this in the past (coherence theory), and (iii) he had failed to heed the advice given in communications courses on the need to put yourself in your listeners' or readers' shoes (pragmatic theory). Learning that particular lesson, and applying it at the next meeting, and at other meetings on different subjects, Jim had further opportunities to check its credibility.

LEARNED BEHAVIOURS

Before leaving credibility checking it is worthwhile drawing attention to one of the facets of *learning orientation* we discussed in Chapter 7, namely learned behaviours. In that chapter we observed that learning orientation, the willingness or openness to learning from experience, depends on three major clusters of personal attributes, namely personality, ability and learned behaviours. The first two are substantially inborn, but the third is something that is acquired from contact with other people, observing their ways of learning.

These were described as 'review procedures, ways of looking back on an event, seeking to note what happened and drawing out the various things that made them happen, and *checking that the lessons learned were reliable*' (page 73). The last seven words are in italics in the present chapter because, of course, they are concerned with credibility checking.

The methods of review procedures, as described in Chapter 7, included post-project reviews, learning logs or diaries and reflective assignments. The first of these are usually in the form of reports which describe what has happened, assess the value of the outcomes and make recommendations for the future. Perhaps the greatest value of such reports is that they are generally the subject of a meeting when their contents are discussed; this enables the sharing of thoughts and the examination of recommendations, so that several minds are brought to bear on the lessons. As we noted in Chapter 9, the sharing of ideas and information has great value in providing different perspectives, and this applies to the processes of credibility checking. Just as someone who is very observant may have much to offer in terms of the data they contribute, someone who is naturally sceptical is likely to push for high standards of scrutiny of the lessons to be learned. One of my colleagues, when looking at a report's recommendations, used to ask himself, and the rest of the meeting, 'how much reliance can we put on these?'. If the answer was a qualified one, perhaps along the lines of 'quite a lot, but the background circumstances were rather special', he would advocate a measure of caution when implementing them.

The lesson I learned from this colleague was the value of a self-critical approach, and this can apply equally to the individual learned behaviours such as learning logs and reflective assignments. The good news is that if you have taken the trouble to write down, in whatever form, your experience(s), perhaps under the headings of the various elements in the Model put forward in this book, it requires relatively little extra effort to ask oneself the question: 'how certain can I be of this?' When Dr Hench (above) was exploring the possible remedies for rheumatoid arthritis, he was receiving very clear answers, initially negative but eventually positive, because he had very clear success criteria. In situations where replication of experiments with slight changes is not possible, for example in Jim's difficult meeting, the answer must necessarily be less certain, but asking it helps to shape the decision on what to do next. In my grass seed experience (Chapter 3), for example, the answer offered by my friend did not seem convincing, and I chose to try again with new seed in the autumn, with good results.

EXPERIENCE BANK

In Chapter 10 we came across our '*own experience*' as a source of data which we can use when making sense of an experience, and the question might reasonably be asked: 'how does our own experience differ from the *experience bank*?'. The answer is 'very little', but it seems to me that the separation is justified in terms of presentation. The element 'own experience' has an entirely legitimate place as a source of data to use when pondering on a new experience, because unless the new experience is almost 'out of this world', a mature adult is likely to have some point of reference against which to compare it. Experience bank is the name for the same element, but in the sequence where it becomes the repository for the lessons or outcomes of an experience.

The Model is already quite complex, as indeed it needs to be in order to cope with quite complex and profound experiences, and to present the two aspects of an individual's experience in one location on the Model would have stretched still further someone's comprehension of the whole. It seems simpler to represent the 'experience bank' as the end point of the sense-making process applied to a given experience, the repository of lessons learned and checked, together, of course, with those conclusions from an experience which do *not* make sense, which we cannot explain (yet), but which have simply to be included in the category of 'puzzles and mysteries of life'. (That there is such a category becomes obvious when we say to ourselves much later something like 'of course – *that's* what was meant by…'.)

Having said this, the content of the experience bank is as described under our own experience in Chapter 10. We noted that it can often subsume much which we originally acquired from formal knowledge, and that it embraces facts, such as hard data, impressions and beliefs, as well as methods and procedures for doing things. At the end of a rich learning experience, any or all of these may be increased in our experience bank, and available, assuming that memory does not let us down, for using in their own right or for helping to make sense of another experience.

POINTS FOR EXPLORATION

The essence of this chapter has been the focus on the question 'how reliable are the insights, learning, or lessons, that we have derived from thinking about an experience?' As a way of exploring this reliability, it would be rewarding to take a few recent experiences and test the lessons we learned from them in the following manner.

Some experiences are capable of replication, so for them the points to explore could be based on Kolb's learning cycle:

- How can I repeat the experience, in different situations, contexts, and so on to test the validity of my learning and lessons?

- To what extent would other people having the same kind of experience come up with similar learning?

Other experiences, however, are not capable of replication, either because the circumstances have changed, or because the experience was so intrinsically dangerous, damaging, or generally unpleasant that repetition could not be contemplated. In these cases, Tony Watson's tests noted above become relevant:

- How do my conclusions *correspond* with what I know about the experience?

- How plausible is it?

- How much reliance can I put on this learning/these lessons, compared with other possible learning/lessons?

Plus, with one eye on the advantages of developing good habits, that is learned behaviours,

- How can I develop a relatively automatic stance of testing my learning from experience?

Finally, and somewhat recurrently, thinking about the above questions could well be helped by talking it through with someone else. So the questions arises:

- Who could help me, and who could I help, in the processes of credibility checking?

CHAPTER 13

Possible Uses for the Model

INTRODUCTION

The preceding nine chapters have been used to describe in a little detail the various elements which are, to varying extents, involved in learning from experience. It is important to recognize, first, that they may come into play in any order or sequence, and second, the whole process is quite likely to be iterative – hence the double arrows in the Model in Figure 3.1. If we are concerned with an *individual's* learning experience, it is probable that the starting point will be the confounding of their expectations and the rousal of emotion of some sort, whereas if the experience is the subject of formal investigation undertaken by a dedicated *group*, such as for the Comet airliner disaster (Chapter 10), the starting point is likely to be the provision of an opportunity as the research team receives its remit and gets down to work. Expectations and emotions will come into play as they gather data from the various sources.

Even quite simple experiences are likely to bring into play the various elements in an iterative manner. For example, if I am walking along a path and feel a sharp pain in the sole of a foot, my *expectation* of a trouble-free walk is disturbed and I feel a strong *emotion* of pain. If I take the opportunity for an immediate examination of the cause I may well find a sharp thorn has penetrated the sole of my trainer, and this prompts a different emotion of surprise, because not only had I not expected thorns on this path but I had thought that the trainer was sufficiently robust to repel any such sharp object. My initial *own observation*, leading to *reflection* and *insight* into the cause of the pain may then lead me to seek for more own observations regarding the number of thorns to be seen on the path, which influences how I walk thereafter. If I have a companion it is likely that *his or her observations*, leading to parallel reflections and insights, will be taken into account. As I reflect on the experience later, I may conclude, after *credibility checking*, that thorns are now an expected hazard and I should walk more carefully, or that I need stronger trainers, or that I should not use that path again, or that it was just bad luck that it happened – very few thorns are that long! The extent to which I persevere with my thinking and observations will depend on my *learning orientation*: for some people such an event will be shrugged off with little or no further thought, others may pay it some attention, while for others it may become obsessive, leading to measurements, surveys and the like. The extent of the learning will vary accordingly.

In this last example the time taken to address the experience and learn from it is pretty well compulsory. For the research group studying the Comet disaster it was their job, while for me the pain caused by the thorn in my foot was so sharp as to demand instant attention. For many less urgent experiences the possibility of learning is optional, and even if it is taken up the results may be only partial compared with what *could* have been learned. So this raises the question – how can the Model be used in a conscious and premeditated way to learn from an experience, and to derive the greatest value from it?

While the answers to this issue are basically the same for both an individual and a group, namely, through the use of self-directed questions, the practicalities are rather different, so they will be discussed separately below. Moreover, because the Model may have something to offer two other areas of individual learning – mentoring and counselling – these too will be discussed separately, albeit more briefly.

INDIVIDUAL LEARNING

The first point to make about an individual's learning from experience is that it is, in very many situations, entirely discretionary, that is it is up to the person to decide for themselves whether to invest the time and energy needed, how much to devote to it, and then how to proceed. There is never enough time for even the most curious person to reflect on *all* the experiences they encounter in their life, so choices must be made – which to focus on, and the extent of the effort to be spent. Two exceptions to this general statement should be made. First, some experiences are so significant for our well-being that paying attention to them is an imperative rather than an option. For example, the thorn in my foot *demands* immediate attention, because if it were allowed to remain my foot could become septic, leading to much more serious problems. Similarly, if we are severely frightened by witnessing the effects of natural phenomena, such as floods or hurricanes, we are likely to organize our lives in such a way as to avoid them. Human beings, like other animals, are so constituted as to examine and learn from experiences which may threaten their existence; as observed in Chapter 11, in the section on processes, we are fascinated by our monsters, that is the things that threaten us, and in so being we are prepared to avoid or defeat them.

Second, on a very different front, we may be *required* by some external agency to explore selected experiences, partly to maximize the learning, the lessons that are available from them, but also to gain some insight into the learning process itself. The argument is that if we are more aware of how we learn, we will be able to do it better. So in external agencies such as universities and colleges, professional bodies and continuous development programmes, syllabi may include what are often called 'learning projects', and 'learning contracts' or 'reflective assignments', where projects, self-selected or given, are used as the basis of self-examination. Assessment in these assignments is usually based not only on the derivation of actual lessons or truths from the work of the assignment itself, but also on evidence of an awareness of how those truths and lessons were derived, and how they could be developed still further.

So, voluntarily or compulsorily, we see a need to dig into an experience with the explicit purpose of learning from it. But how? The answer lies in the Model, each element of which offers some evidence of how we learn. At the end of each of the earlier chapters which is concerned with one or more of the elements is a section headed the 'Points for exploration' in which are posed a number of self-directed questions intended to open up particular facets of the experience, and in this chapter, when answering the question 'how to dig into an experience?', it is worthwhile revisiting them.

Note: If at all possible, it will work to your advantage if you can take time when pondering these questions. As we saw in the processes section of Chapter 11, 'incubation' is often an important ingredient in sense-making. It is generally helpful to have a first shot at answering them, and then another, say, a day later.

ELEMENT A – EXPECTATIONS

The disruption of your expectations is often the first sign that an experience has some lessons to offer. So self-directed questions like the following help to open up the subject:

- What were my expectations before the event? What led me to them? NB Remember that, as we saw in Chapter 4, expectations may be in 'default' mode, that is we expect that things will continue unchanged. A meeting, someone's response or behaviour, what actually happened in an incident, would be as they have been in the past.

- If the event or experience lasted some time, for example several days or longer, how did my expectations change and develop? What events led to these changes?

- How would my expectations change in the light of the experience?

ELEMENT B – EMOTIONS

Emotions follow closely after expectations. As we saw in Chapter 5, emotions convey information, both to ourselves and other people. So if we are frightened, shocked, surprised, delighted, or whatever, these emotions are worth noting so that we can explore why we felt that way. Typical questions include:

- What emotion(s) did I feel at the start of the experience?

- How did they change as the experience/event unfolded?

- What were these emotions telling me about what I would have to be doing in the future?

ELEMENT C – OPPORTUNITY

If you are reading this in order to receive a little inspiration on how to make sense of an experience, you clearly have made an opportunity for reflection or some sort of thought! Useful first questions could include:

- How can I make time, that is create opportunities, to consider this experience further? (Chapter 6 quotes some examples, but they are not exhaustive.)

- Who do I need to influence (if anyone) to help in this?

Chapter 6 mentioned the open questions, what?, how?, why?, and so on, which often open up the experience, and examples of typical self-directed questions are:

- What exactly was the experience? Describe it as fully as possible.

- Why am I devoting time to this reflection? Examples of answers could include: in order to avoid such a painful experience in the future; to understand my colleague X better; to write a convincing account of learning from experience; in order to increase the satisfaction from the experience.

- Who can help me, that is, who shared the experience, or understands it?

- What other sources of information on it are there?

- How can I work on this experience most effectively?

ELEMENT D – LEARNING ORIENTATION

An individual's learning orientation is that unique, but changing, combination of personality, ability (developed intelligence), and learned behaviours. Given that in this section we are looking at *individual learning*, the issue which arises for someone reflecting on a new experience is: what is *my* learning orientation? And from this, how can it be harnessed most effectively to learn from this experience? The three components of learning orientation are:

PERSONALITY

While our personality is deeply rooted and unlikely to change significantly throughout our lives, our *behaviour* can, if required, be uncharacteristic of our personality. For example, if someone is naturally shy and withdrawn they may be able, nevertheless, if the occasion demands it, put on a performance of being outgoing and extrovert. It would put such a person under great strain to be outgoing and extrovert all the time, but for short periods, hosting a reception, perhaps, it would be quite possible. So as part of the 'digging into an experience' process, it makes sense to review your personality in order to see where its strengths contribute to the process, and whether other means can be found for overcoming its limitations. Therefore:

- What do I know of my personality from external sources, such as Myers-Briggs Types, Honey and Mumford's Learning Styles, and so on?

- Have I a trusted companion/colleague whom I could rely on to give as objective an appraisal as possible, and if so, what would they say?

- When I look at other people whose personalities seem helpful for the 'digging into experience process' what do I see? In other words, what makes them successful?

- In the light of the above, what changes in my behaviour could be indicated, even if they are deployed infrequently?

NB The good news is that this self-analysis work is needed only occasionally, and once attempted need not be repeated for every experience. It is probably a good idea to repeat it every few years.

ABILITY

The same exercise just described for personality could be repeated, for ability, using the seven-intelligence framework based on Gardner's work. The difference here, however, is that abilities are much more focused on those needed to explore a *particular* experience. For example, a particular project experience could require, amongst other skills, some facility with statistics, in which case one could consult a book on statistics, or seek advice from a statistician. So the questions for a particular experience could be:

- To make sense of this particular experience, what abilities are needed?

- How strong am I in them?

- If the answer is 'not very strong', what can I do to make good this shortfall?

Again, it makes good sense to invite a colleague's assessment of your strengths and limitations, and consider with them ways of making good the latter.

LEARNED BEHAVIOURS

These are essentially review procedures, so the 'digging into experience' process is a matter of applying your established methods – and possibly developing new ones. There are some examples in the relevant section of Chapter 7. One of the merits of this approach is that it is systematic, so that, provided a review procedure is comprehensive, using it will cover all the angles.

ELEMENT D – MEMORY

As we saw in Chapter 8, memory is significant in learning from experience in at least two respects. The more aspects and details of an experience that we can remember the more reliable are the lessons to be derived from it. Placing this experience alongside other similar experiences we have encountered previously provides a richer and fuller set of data on which to reflect, and again leads to more reliable lessons.

So the question is: how can we help to keep it fresh and accurate? Two methods have been tried, tested and proved effective. First, *write it down*. Taking notes, if possible while the experience is unfolding, provides an excellent memory jogger when you come to ponder and seek to make sense of it later on. If it is not possible to make notes during the action, write them down as soon as possible afterwards. After leaving a meeting with a customer, one of my colleagues used to sit in the car park and jot down everything he could recall. Notes need not be long. For many years I have found that mind maps, mentioned in Chapter 6, are excellent vehicles for recalling different facets of an experience; the various elements in the Model provide convenient pegs on which to hang single words or phrases which encompass different facets.

The second aid to good memory retention is *telling someone else*. We saw in Chapter 8 that the key to remember something is by revising it at extending intervals after it has been learned, and telling is revising. So if you could contrive to give an account of an experience to different people on the day it happened, one day later, one week later, one month later, after six months and after one year, you would probably remember that experience for the rest of your life!

ELEMENTS E, F, AND G

You, personally, will generally provide the greater part of the observable data on your experience, so it is a matter of ensuring that you capture it as fully as possible. Kipling's questions provide an excellent vehicle for achieving this:

- What did I see/hear/, and so on?

- Who said/did …?

- When did it happen?

- Why did it happen?

- What was its background?

And so on. Your expectations and emotions will probably have been noted earlier, but if not they, too, are worth recording as part of the overall experience.

Moreover, as said in the boxed note earlier in this chapter on uses for the Model, it is worth *taking time* to answer these questions. Allowing yourself a second, and even a third, opportunity to answer your self-directed questions often yields further, useful information.

Never overlook the possibility of other people contributing to your data. Colleagues may have been present, bystanders around, and participants in the experience itself – they all may have things to add which contribute to explanations, and thus to the possible lessons.

- As with self-directed questions, ask open questions, inviting full answers rather than a confirmatory yes or no.

- Don't neglect the 'informed non-participant'. He or she, although not present in the experience, may suggest ways of looking at it, other questions to ask, and even explanations.

ELEMENTS H AND J – FORMAL KNOWLEDGE AND OUR OWN EXPERIENCE

As a generalization, most experiences will draw on either formal knowledge or our own experience. Highly personal experiences, such as being a witness to an almost violent argument or a close encounter with a near-disaster, tend to draw on our own experience, when we compare and contrast the current event with others of a similar kind in our past. Unless we are students of behavioural psychology we are unlikely to draw on written material on extreme behaviour when seeking to understand what happened in a violent argument; rather we recall any earlier situations and look for common features, trends or sequences which explain what was happening. On the other hand, when required to investigate an experience in which we had no part, we are more likely to look for data which is in the public domain, or, like the Comet air disaster investigators, carry out experiments which add to the knowledge in the public domain.

So for *impersonal* experiences, the question is likely to be:

- What is in the public domain that can help me?

- Where can I find it?

- Who can help me find it, and understand it?

ELEMENTS K AND L – REFLECTION AND INSIGHT

In the chapter on reflection and insight we analysed the various activities of sense-making into prompts, processes and products, and this structure will be followed below.

PROMPTS

As we saw earlier, an individual's need to learn from an experience is usually rooted in the dissonance or discrepancy between what we expected and what actually happened, and our need to reduce that dissonance. This could be seen as an 'informal' need. The other, more 'formal' reason for learning, comes from a requirement from an external agent, for example when, in public life, a body is set up to enquire into the causes of a disaster so that it can be avoided in future, or when, as part of a formal academic course, a project is used as a learning assignment. In both these situations it is worthwhile asking the questions of oneself:

- What am I hoping to achieve?

- How can I achieve it as comprehensively and quickly as possible?

In the formal setting the answer to the question: why am I doing this? is obvious, namely to meet a requirement, but this does not remove the self-obligation to use one's intelligence when carrying out the requirement. The formal remit of an investigation might not be worded in such a way as to elicit all the relevant lessons, and it is implicit – although not always explicit – in learning assignments that one's own ways of learning are also important subjects for reflection and insight, as well as lessons derived from the project. The question *'why am I doing this?* prompts consideration of the spirit of the study as well as the letter.

For informal sense-making, the questions are helpful in ensuring clarity of purpose. In the text-box illustrations earlier in the book the purposes were always clear, generally relating to the avoidance of dissonance and the improvement of future performance (they were chosen for that reason), but very often as life moves on and experiences which at one time demanded elucidation and offered good value in terms of effort and results, diminish in attractiveness, being supplanted by others.

PROCESSES

In Chapter 11 we saw that, in our attempts to reduce cognitive dissonance, various ways were used to make sense of experiences. (The list was not presented as comprehensive, but as those used by my research colleagues, and drawn from the literature.) Those ways entail different approaches to experience, and the following questions and observations are offered as 'starters' to focus initial thinking.

- How, if at all, will pure logic help me (deductive and inductive reasoning)?

- Is the project/experience embedded in a wider organizational issue in which systems thinking would help? If so, where can I find out about it?

- To what extent is this experience part of a pattern?

- How can changing my perspective on the experience help, for example by adopting the position of another participant?

- If hoping for sudden insight, a 'eureka', remember that it would need to be preceded by plenty of hard work and a period of incubation.

- If time and opportunity prevent you understanding it fully, a 'rule of thumb' might provide an adequate outcome. It would be important to recognize it as such.

- And if all else fails, register the experience as a paradox, an inexplicable. It is quite possible that later on, after months or even years, more data and reflection may yield some insight.

PRODUCTS

In Chapter 11 the possible 'outcomes' of experiential learning were presented as a spectrum, from knowledge, through understanding and judgement, to skills, and it is worthwhile taking a little time to consider where your conclusions on an experience fit. It is quite possible that they will cover several parts, for example: a project may yield a number of facts – knowledge; an awareness of how things fit together – understanding; some sensing of priorities when working through the project – judgement; and the acquisition of some facility and techniques when doing so – skills.

ELEMENT M – CREDIBILITY CHECKING

The example of credibility checking given in Chapter 12, Dr Hench's discovery of cortisone, was a clear-cut instance of a series of checks, initially giving negative results but finally positive, albeit with severe limitations for Hench's original objective in the treatment of rheumatoid arthritis. This type of science-based study is based on the logic of inductive reasoning, and is intended to give clear results which are as unequivocal as possible. By the same token, some projects can be constructed in such a way that similarly transparent results are the outcome, and credibility checking is relatively straightforward.

However, many other experiences, arguably *most* experiences which have an element of human interaction, are not as straightforward, and in these cases Tony Watson's approach is commended. So, referring back to the section on 'Other forms of credibility checking' in Chapter 12, the self-directed questions would be along the following lines:

- To what extent do the outcome(s) *correspond* with the data gathered?

- How *plausible* are the outcomes, given the known background as revealed by the gathered data?

- If there is a choice between possible outcomes, taking a *pragmatic* approach, which seems most likely to lead to successful action?

Finally, credibility checking can be 'institutionalized' when it is built into the review procedures discussed under 'Learned behaviours'. Good, robust procedures will include towards the end some type of self-directed question along the lines of 'how certain can I be of this?', and the development of such a procedure could be one of the very best outcomes of a reflective assignment. The important thing is to do your own self-criticism – before others do it for you!

GROUP LEARNING

It will be obvious that the learning from an experience, a project, a success, a disaster, or some other event, which can be undertaken by a group could follow essentially the same lines as that described for an individual above. The Model provides a method of approach, and the technique is primarily one of framing and answering self-addressed questions similar to those offered above for individuals.

Because a group consists of two or more individuals, however, there will be some advantages and some potential drawbacks compared with the sole individual's learning. Some advantages:

- there will be some variety of *expectations* and *emotions*; indeed, four individuals in a group might well have four sets of expectations and emotions

- there is also likely to be an increase in '*own observations*'

- there will be potential for division of labour. Different *learning orientations* will probably bring different abilities, and perhaps some different personality traits, for example resilience and perseverance.

On the other hand, there may be a need to spend time seeking clarity of purpose for the project. Time spent at the start discussing what the remit really means, and how it can be achieved, will be well spent. Consequently, it may take a little longer than if one person is carrying it out, but the outcomes should be better.

The dynamics of learning from each other within a group, and of sharing of lessons, whether by groups or individuals, is an interesting process. It seems to me that there is a danger of confining the sharing to observations and the actual lessons themselves. Thus someone might speak, or write, along the lines of: in situation ABC the lessons I learned were XYZ. This is probably an over-cerebral process for many people to relate to. We saw much earlier that individual learning from experience is usually triggered by the confounding of expectations and the stimulation of emotion, and that the purpose of emotion is to convey information – to others and to ourselves.

If the listeners to our observations and lessons, whether individuals or groups, are to internalize them and be willing to act on them, they should also hear something of what motivated our learning in the first place. If Jim had confined his account of his exceptional learning event to its outcomes in terms of the importance of how his messages would be received, his contribution would have been far less memorable. But his account was very different; he said, in effect, 'I expected that the union lads would accept my arguments, but they didn't – and I was gutted!' He conveyed the extent of the shattering of his expectations – 'they countered [my arguments] and they countered them very well', whilst his emotions were raw – 'I was crucified! I was made to look a gibbering idiot.' Most listeners would empathize with Jim when he talked like that, and from that fellow-feeling they could move on to hear how he was able to dig himself out of his self-dug pit.

For some people, putting their emotions on show can be embarrassing, almost painful, and yet if our purpose is to encourage a change in behaviour by applying the lessons we have learned, our chances of success are much greater if we are prepared to share the whole story, not just the happy ending. Our position could perhaps be something along the lines of: 'In order to understand what I learned from this experience you need to know how it hit me at the outset, how my expectations were not met, and how this left me feeling.'

An interesting account of group learning, and the transference of group learning, is given in a *Harvard Business Review* article on a US Army training unit called OPFOR (Operating Force).[1] OPFOR is a brigade whose job is to prepare active soldiers by fighting a succession of fresh brigades in training manoeuvres in a wide variety of different combat situations – open country, street to street, terrorist strikes and so on. The opposing force in any encounter, always called Blue Force (BLUFOR), has the same initial briefing, but the secret of OPFOR's success – it nearly always wins – is the depth of its 'after-action review' (AAR), a version of the review procedures discussed in Chapter 7 on learning orientation. AARs, or post-project reviews, are fairly common in many organizations, but what makes OPFFORs practice distinctive, and highly effective, according to the writers, is that 'OPFOR treats every action as an opportunity for learning – about what to do but also, more important, about how to think'. The authors say that AARs should be 'more verb than noun – a living pervasive process that explicitly connects past experience with future action' (Darling, Parry and Moore, 2005, page 87).

Moreover, OPFOR illustrates the importance of the 'respectful interaction' quoted in Chapter 9 as being essential for the sharing of data. They have 'house rules', quoted at the start of every AAR:

---

1   'Learning in the thick of it' by Darling, Parry and Moore (2005).

- participate

- no thin skins

- leave your stripes at the door

- take notes

- focus on our issues, not the issues of those above us

- absolute candour (senior leaders are first to acknowledge their own mistakes)

- focus on improving performance, not placing blame (Darling, Parry and Moore, 2005, page 88).

As part of the training process, OPFOR makes a point of sharing the lessons it draws out from its encounters with successive BLUFORs, but it usually wins because it learns its lessons more effectively.

MENTORING AND COUNSELLING

This is not a book on either of these subjects, but when I have been discussing the Model with colleagues it has been suggested that it may have something to offer both activities. Several people have suggested that the informed non-participant is an alias for a mentor, not to mention coaches and instructors – which seems to be a comment on the elastic nature of some of these terms.

MENTORING

True mentoring, as described by an authority such as David Clutterbuck,[2] encompasses a wider set of activities and relationships with the learner than is envisaged in the Model. The Model is constructed with generalized learning in mind, from, hypothetically, one experience or event, whereas mentoring implies an ongoing, almost permanent, relationship between mentor and learner.[3] During the course of seeking to learn from an experience, the experiential learner might well approach several – even many – different informed non-participants, each being qualified in one aspect of the experience, whereas it

2   See *Everyone Needs a Mentor* (2001) by David Clutterbuck.
3   Chapter 3 discusses different models of mentoring, and compares it with teaching, tutoring and coaching, and on page 26 there is a line by line comparison with coaching.

would be normal practice for a mentor's learner to have one, or at the most two or three, mentors at a time.

Having said this, the Model may be of help to mentors in providing a model, or even a checklist, to use when helping their learners. The basic role of a mentor is to help the development, using the term in its broadest sense, of the learner, and the Model offers, for one or for successive experiences, a way of approaching this development. Clutterbuck points out that mentoring 'emphasises feedback and reflection by the learner', and that the mentor and learner 'typically [have] a longer-term relationship, often for "life"'.[4] The Model offers several entry points to nourish that relationship.

COUNSELLING

In the same vein, the Model could provide a framework for a counsellor or helper and their client to work through when seeking to understand what has happened in the past, and what it could mean for the future.

The term 'counselling' covers a very wide span of activities, and addresses an even wider range of human conditions, from those in which someone is in the utter depths of despair, possibly following a personal tragedy, through to an exploration of future career options. Accordingly, the aims of counsellors when working with clients are varied, but typically include the following: insight, relating with others, self-awareness, self-acceptance, enlightenment, acquisition of social skills, change (cognitive, behavioural, systemic) and empowerment.[5]

Just as counselling aims imply a broad spectrum of activities, the professionalism of counsellors is also very broad. At one extreme would be medically trained psychiatrists and psychotherapists, dealing with profound mental problems; in the mid-range would be professionally qualified counsellors dealing with, for example, marriage and social problems, whilst at the other extreme are 'helpers', a 'generic term to cover all those engaged in using counselling and helping skills'.[6] Richard Nelson-Jones, in his book *Basic Counselling Skills: A Helper's Manual* describes helpers as:

---

4   Page 26, Table 2 this volume.
5   See *An Introduction to Counselling* (2003) by John McLeod. This list is taken from pages 12–13, where he makes the point that it is unlikely that a counsellor would attempt all the aims listed, at least with any one client, but it serves to show the breadth of counselling work.
6   Gerard Egan in *Skilled Helper* (2002).

para-professional or quasi-counsellors who use counselling skills as
part of other primary roles ... voluntary counselling and helping, and
those who participate in peer helping and support networks.

(2003, page 6)

Clearly, I have in mind the 'helper' end of the spectrum when suggesting that
the Model could be of relevance. Several of the aims of counselling set out in
the paragraph above accord with the Model's elements. For example, in inviting
the client to explore their emotions, and quite possibly the personality aspects
of their learning orientation, the counsellor/helper could shape a dialogue out
of which the client would hopefully gain some understanding of the issues
which concern them. An exploration of a client's expectations of a troublesome
experience, and of how the client might perceive other people's view of that
experience, could lead to insight from which the client could work toward
some sort of accommodation.

Bibliography

Averill, JR (1997) 'The emotions: an integrative approach' in R Hogan, J Johnson, and S Briggs (eds) *Handbook of Personality Psychology*, Academic Press, San Diego, CA.

Baddeley, AD (1999) *Essentials of Human Memory*, Psychology Press, Hove.

Baker, A, Jensen, P and Kolb, DA (2002) *Conversational Learning: An experiential approach to knowledge creation*, Quorum Books, Westport, CT.

Bayne, R (1997) *The Myers-Briggs Type Indicator*, reprinted in 2002 by Nelson Thornes, Cheltenham.

Beevor, A (2005) 'You answer the questions', *Independent*, 21 October.

Blakemore, C (1988) *The Mind Machine*, BBC Books, London.

Boden, MA (2004) *The Creative Mind: Myths and Mechanisms*, Routledge, London.

Boud, D (2006) 'Creating the space for reflection', in D Boud, P Cressey and P Docherty (eds) *Productive Reflection at Work*, Routledge, Abingdon.

Boud, D, Keogh, R and Walker, D (1985) 'Promoting reflection in learning: a model', in D Boud, R Keogh and D Walker, *Reflection: Turning Experience into Learning*, Kogan Page, London.

Boud, D, Cressey, P, and Docherty, P (2006) *Productive Reflection at Work*, Routledge, Abingdon.

Bragg, M (2003) *The Adventure of English – 500AD to 2000AD: The biography of a language*, Hodder and Stoughton, London.

Briggs Myers, I (1995) *Gifts Differing*, Davies-Black, Mountain View, CA.

Brunner, LS and Suddarth, DS (1989) *The Lippincott Manual of Medical-Surgical Nursing*, Harper and Row, London.

Bryman, A (1988) *Quantity and Quality in Social Research*, Routledge, London.

Buzan, T (1982) *Use Your Head*, BBC Books, London.

Buzan, T (2003) *Using Your Memory*, BBC Books, London.

Buzan, T (2005) *The Ultimate Book of Mind Maps*, Thorsons, Harper Collins, London.

Chesterton, G (2005) 'No turning back',*Independent on Sunday*, 26 June 2005.

Clore, GC (1994) 'Why emotions are felt', in P Ekman and RJ Davidson (eds) *The Nature of Emotions*, Oxford University Press, New York.

Clutterbuck, D (2001) *Everyone Needs a Mentor*, CIPD, London.

Cortese, CG (2005) 'Learning through Teaching', *Management Learning* 36(1).

Csikszentmihalyi, M (1996) *Creativity*, HarperCollins, New York.

Csikszentmihalyi, M and Sawyer, K (1995) 'Creative insight: The social dimension of a solitary moment', in RJ Sternbergand and JE Davidson (eds) *The Nature of Insight*, Bradford Books, MIT Press, Cambridge MA.

Darling, M, Parry, C and Moore, J (2005) 'Learning in the thick of it', *Harvard Business Review* (July–August).

Davies, JML (2002) *How Experienced Managers Learn from Exceptional Events*, PhD thesis, Lancaster University.

Davies, L and Kraus, P (2003) 'Individual learning from exceptional events' in M Lee (ed.) *HRD in a Complex World,* Routledge, London.

Derksen, K, Keursten, P and Streuner, J (2007) 'Management by co-creation' in Rosemary Hill and Jim Stewart (eds) *Management Development: Perspectives from research and practice*, Routledge, Abingdon.

Egan, G (2002) *Skilled Helper*, Wadsworth, London.

Festinger, L (1957) *A Theory of Cognitive Dissonance*, Stanford UP, Stanford CA.

Gardner, H (1993) *Frames of Mind: The Theory of Multiple Intelligences*, Fontana, London.

Gardner, H (1999) *Intelligence Reframed: Multiple Intelligences for the 21st Century*, Basic Books, New York.

Garnham, A and Oakhill, J (1994) *Thinking and Reasoning*, Blackwell, Oxford.

Gold, J, Thorpe, R and Holt, R (2007) 'Writing, reading and reason' in R Hill and J Stewart (eds) *Management Development: Perspectives from research and practice*, Routledge, Abingdon.

Hadamard, J (1949) *The Psychology of Invention in the Mathematical Field*, Princeton University Press, Princeton, NJ.

Hampson, S (1999) 'State of the art: Personality', *The Psychologist* 12(6).

Hewett, C (2004) 'Larder puts the case for England's defence', *Independent*, 21 February.

Honderich, T (1995) *The Oxford Companion to Philosophy*, Oxford University Press, New York.

Honey, P and Mumford, A (1986) *The Manual of Learning Styles*, Honey, Maidenhead.

Hornyak, MJ, Green, SG and Heppard, KA (2007) 'Implementing experiential learning: it's not rocket science' in M Reynolds and R Vince (eds) *The Handbook of Experiential Learning and Management Education*, Oxford University Press, Oxford.

Jarvis, P (1994) 'Learning practical knowledge', *JFHE*, 18(1).

Jung-Beeman, M *et al.* (2004) 'Neural activity when people solve verbal problems in insight', *PLOS Biology*, 2(4).

Kayes, AB (2007) 'Power and experience: emancipation through guided leadership narratives', in M Reynolds and R Vincev (eds) *The Handbook of Experiential Learning and Management Education*, Oxford University Press, Oxford.

Keursten, P and Streuner, J (2007) 'Management by co-creation' in Rosemary Hill and Jim Stewart (eds) *Management Development: Perspectives from research and practice*, Routledge, Abingdon.

Kitchener, KS and Brenner, HG (1990) 'Wisdom and reflective judgement; knowing in the face of uncertainty', in R Sternberg (ed.) *Wisdom: Its origins, nature and development*, Cambridge University Press, Cambridge.

Kolb, DA (1984) *Experiential Learning*, Prentice-Hall, Englewood Cliffs, NJ.

Le Fanu, J (2000) *The Rise and Fall of Modern Medicine*, Abacus, London.

Lee, Monica (Ed.) (2003) *HRD in a Complex World*, Routledge, London.

Louis, MR and Sutton RI (1991) 'Switching cognitive gears: From habits of mind to active thinking', *Human Relations*, 44(1).

Lincoln, YS and Guba, EG (1985) *Naturalistic Inquiry*, Sage, London.

Marshall, SP (1995) *Schemas in Problem Solving*, Cambridge University Press, Cambridge.

McCrae, RR and Costa, PT (1997) 'Conceptions and correlates of openness to experience,' in RR Hogan, J Johnson and S Briggs (eds) *Handbook of Personality Psychology*, Academia Press, San Diego, CA.

McGreevy, AL (2004) 'Under her spell: An analysis of the creativity of JK Rowling', *Gifted Education International* 19(1).

McLeod, J (2003) *An Introduction to Counselling*, Open University Press, Maidenhead.

Menand, L (2002) *The Metaphysical Club*, Flamingo, HarperCollins, London.

Mezirow, J (1991) *Transformative Dimensions of Adult Learning*, Jossey-Bass, San Francisco.

Moon, J (1999) *Reflection in Learning and Professional Development*, Kogan Page, London.

Nelson-Jones, R (2003) *Basic Counselling Skills*, Sage, London.

O'Connor, J and McDermott, I (1997) *The Art of Systems Thinking*, Thorsons, London.

O'Connor, J and Seymour, J (1993) *Introducing NLP*, Aquarian Press, London

Pervin, LA and John, OJ (2001) *Personality*, Wiley, New York.

Proust, M (1923) *La Prisonière*, translated as *The Captive*, by CK Scott Moncrieff, Knopf, London.

Ramachandran, VS and Blakeslee, S (1998) *Phantoms in the Brain*, Fourth Estate, London.

Reber, AS (1995) *Dictionary of Psychology*, Penguin Books, London.

Reynolds, M (1997) 'Learning styles: A critique', *Management Learning* 28(2).

Reynolds, M (1998) 'Reflection and critical reflection in management learning', *Management Learning*, 29(2).

Sartre, J-P (1947) *Huis Clos*, Gallimard, Paris.

Schön, DA (1983) *The Reflective Practitioner*, Arena Books, Aldershot.

Summers, A and Swan, R (2005) *Sinatra: The life*, Doubleday, London.

Syk, A (2004) 'The learning curve', *History Today*, November, 12–19.

Watson, TJ (2001) *Organising and Managing Work: Organisation, Managerial and Strategic Behaviour in Theory and Practice*, FT Prentice Hall, Harlow.

Wearing, D (2005) *Forever Today*, Doubleday, London.

Weick, KE (1993) 'The collapse of sense-making in organisations: the Mann Gulch disaster', *Administrative Science Quarterly*, 38.

Weick, KE (1995) *Sensemaking in Organisations*, Sage, Thousand Oaks, CA.

White, J (1998) *Do Howard Gardener's multiple intelligences add up?* Institute of Education, University of London.

Wilson, Edward O (1978) *On Human Nature*, Harvard University Press, Cambridge, MA.

Index

Printed in Great Britain
by Amazon